Stories
That Teach
Gospel
Principles

Stories
That Teach
Gospel
Principles

Allan K. Burgess
Max H. Molgard

Bookcraft
Salt Lake City, Utah

Library of Congress Catalog Card Number: 89-61162

ISBN 0-88494-701-7

First Printing, 1989

Printed in the United States of America

Our thanks to those who were willing to share their experiences with us so that we could in turn share them with others.

Contents

Contents

Introduction

The basic purpose of this book is to help parents and teachers have a reliable source of true stories that can enrich home evenings, Church lessons, talks, and personal study.

This book contains both a subject and a scripture index. If you were preparing a lesson on faith, you could use the subject index to see which stories teach faith. If you were preparing a lesson on 1 Nephi 3:7, you could use the scripture index to see if there are stories that enrich that particular passage of scripture. An effort has been made to choose scriptures that closely correlate with the stories.

A chapter has been included that gives ideas for making stories more effective. Also, at the end of each story is a section called "Teaching Ideas and Related Scriptures" which gives added help in making the stories more powerful.

Ideas for Making Stories More Effective

Few things catch our attention quicker and hold it better than a good story. The Savior used stories and examples to illustrate and apply his teachings over and over again.

Whether we are using a story to illustrate a point, springboard into a lesson, or help apply some gospel principle, there are some things that we can do to make stories more effective. Many teachers have found that the following ideas have made a significant difference in their use of stories.

Tell Instead of Read

Most stories are much more effective when we tell them instead of read them. When telling a story, we have a chance to put our own personality into the story while maintaining eye-to-eye contact with those we are teaching. We can walk around, gesture with our hands and body, use facial expressions, and make the story seem so much more personal and alive.

It's really quite simple to prepare ourselves to tell a story instead of reading it. First, we should read the story two or three times. It helps to read it out loud, emphasizing those areas that we feel strongest about. The second step is to tell the story, out loud, in our own words. This can be to another person, to the wall, or even to the dog. If there is some part of the story that we can't remember, we then should reread that part and tell the story again. With most stories, this is all it takes to make the story our own. If the story is fairly complicated, we can make a brief outline of the story as a guide. Usually by the time we are going to use the story, we no longer need the outline.

Read Part of the Story

Some stories have certain sections that are written in such a way that it is difficult to tell the whole story and be as effective. With these stories we have found it very successful to tell most of the story line and read the two or three sections that pack great power just the way they are written. This works especially well with longer stories that may not hold people's attention if the whole stories are read.

Reading the Story

If we have decided to read the story, and if it is possible, it nearly always works better to have copies so everyone can read along. Of course, this isn't possible in many settings, but it does seem to make most stories more effective and interesting. When others can read along, they concentrate better than when they are just listening. Also, more learning seems to take place when we read something as well as hear it.

Make Sure of the Source

Many stories are passed around by word of mouth that are not true. Many others have even been written down and circulated from friend to friend and from ward to ward. When we were compiling this book, one of our concerns was that we verify each story's validity. Every story in the book comes from someone that was personally involved in it and has a history of honesty and integrity.

We taught a class for fifty gospel teachers a few years ago and told them a very inspirational story about a religious leader who had joined the LDS Church and who subsequently was the instrument in the conversion of thousands of people. It was a very impressive story, and, after telling it to the teachers, we asked how many of them would like a copy of it so they could share it with their students. Every teacher in the class enthusiastically raised his hand; not one of them asked about the source of the story. We explained to them that the story had been circulated throughout the Church and was completely false. We then had an opportunity to teach them the importance of double-checking the source of questionable stories before they passed them on to others. We need to be especially careful of sharing stories that are passed from person to person or have been copied off on handouts but have no reference of any kind.

Use Open-Ended Stories

Few teaching methods get people more involved in a lesson than open-ended stories. Many of the stories in this book could be used in this way. The idea is to tell the first part of the story and then invite the class to decide what the person in the story should do and what they think he really does. This can be done with questions or even sharing together some quotations and scriptures that clarify what the person should do. Once the class has decided what should be done and what they think the person actually does, finish telling the story. You can then easily apply the principles in the story to your students' lives.

Use Questions

Questions can be used throughout the telling or reading of a story to keep everyone involved and thinking. Many of these questions do not need to be answered verbally as long as those listening are thinking about the answers. Some examples of questions that might be used are: "What would you do in this situation?" "What do you think she will do next?" "Is that what you would have done?" "What do you think Heavenly Father would like her to do?" "Why do you think she did that?"

Ideas for Involving Young People

1. Use puppets. Have a puppet tell the story or put on a puppet show with the story. (You can use simple puppets such as finger puppets, lunch sack puppets with yarn for hair, or shadow puppets.)

2. Make flannel board pieces or, better yet, have your children make them. Then use these pieces as you tell the story. (Needed materials include Pellon, crayons, paper, and masking tape.)

3. Assign different parts in the story to class or family members and have them read or tell their part.

4. Have the students dress up and act out the story. By the time they practice several times, they will know the story well. If a video camera is available, you can film the story and view it over and over again.

5. Use objects. Make or gather them ahead of time for use during the story, or you can tell the story first and then make or draw something that the story talked about (such as staffs, stones, slings, Lehi's tent, Liahona, ark, boat, Goliath, Moroni's title of liberty, etc.).

6. Have each person prepare ahead of time part of the story and tell it in their own words.

7. Have young children assigned to do sound effects at the right times. You can point at them each time you want their sound effect. Think of how much fun you would have with a story like Noah and the flood.

8. Make an audio tape of the story. Involve the class with sound effects and in telling the story. The children will listen to the story over and over again.

I Want to Be Your Friend

And be ye kind one to another, tenderhearted, forgiving one another, even as God for Christ's sake hath forgiven you.

Ephesians 4:32

Tommy was one of the most difficult third-grade students the school had ever worked with. He was cross-eyed, dirty, and seemed to very seldom take a bath so he usually had very bad body odor. His gym shoes were tied together with string and his clothes were soiled and wrinkled. Many of the students taunted him and called him all kinds of names like "Stinky" and "Cross-eyes."

The teacher wondered what kind of parents would send Tommy to school this way, so she visited his house. It wasn't a house really; it was more like a large shack at the end of a dirt road. She found that Tommy's mother had died and that the father had a very low income and worked long hours. It was a very large family and there just wasn't enough money to go around. They had no hot water or electricity in their home, and, while the teacher was there, an older sister was washing the family clothes in a tub filled with cold water in the center of the room. She didn't even have any soap to help get the clothes clean.

Tommy had no friends and he went to great lengths to try to show the other children that it didn't matter to him. Some days he would stand on his desk and tell the children in his class that he hated them before he would sit down. He refused to go outside for recess or lunch because this is when the other children were the most cruel to him.

The teacher tried everything she could think of to get Tommy and the other children to accept each other, but nothing seemed to work. Then she thought of William. William was one of the best third-grade students in the school and was in the same class as Tommy. The other children looked up to him, and he always seemed very kind and considerate. Maybe if she could somehow get Tommy and William to be friends, the rest of the class would fall into place.

She went to William and talked to him in private. She told him a little about Tommy and how much he needed a friend. She then asked him if he would be willing to try to be friends with Tommy, even if Tommy didn't want to be friends. He said that he would give it a try.

When it was time for recess, William went up to Tommy and asked him to go out and play with him. Tommy said that he didn't want to play with him and slugged William right in the nose. The blow knocked him to the floor. That would have been enough for most people, but William got up and said, "I don't care what you do to me; I'm going to be your friend." Tommy retorted that he didn't want a friend and knocked him to the floor again. William jumped up and approached Tommy the third time and, for the third time, hit the floor. But William would not quit—and the fourth time was different. When William said for the fourth time that he was going to be Tommy's friend, Tommy believed him, and friends they became.

From that time on, Tommy was a much happier person. He still had some problems and some learning disabilities, but once William became his friend, a few other children did also. It didn't take long for most of the children in the class to quit teasing Tommy and look for something more fun to do.

Teaching Ideas and Related Scriptures

Forgiveness: William was willing to forgive Tommy as many times as he needed in order to become his friend instead of his enemy.

D&C 64:10. "I, the Lord, will forgive whom I will forgive, but of you it is required to forgive all men." (*See also* Matthew 5:44;

Matthew 18:21-22; Ephesians 4:32; 1 Peter 3:8-9; 3 Nephi 13:14-15.)

Judging Others: The teacher found herself judging Tommy's mother for the way she sent him to school. She didn't know that Tommy's mother was dead. The children judged Tommy as a person of no worth because of his appearance, even though every person on earth is a son or daughter of God and of great worth.

Matthew 7:1-2. "Judge not, that ye be not judged.

"For with what judgment ye judge, ye shall be judged: and with what measure ye mete, it shall be measured to you again." (*See also* 1 Samuel 16:7; John 7:24; Moroni 7:18.)

Kindness: All of us need to show the kindness that William did to those who may be different in some way. Sometimes we are so afraid of what others may think of us if we become friends with an outcast that we forget how good God feels about us when we show kindness and become friends.

Ephesians 4:32. "And be ye kind one to another, tender-hearted, forgiving one another, even as God for Christ's sake hath forgiven you." (*See also* Matthew 7:12; 1 Nephi 19:9; Moroni 7:45.)

Love: William gave us a perfect example of what can happen when we love our enemies. Most of the time we lose an enemy and gain a friend.

John 13:34-35. "A new commandment I give unto you, That ye love one another; as I have loved you, that ye also love one another.

"By this shall all men know that ye are my disciples, if ye have love one to another." (*See also* Matthew 5:43-47; John 3:16; 1 Peter 3:8-9; Moroni 7:45, 47-48.)

You Can't Make Me Dishonest for Ten Dollars

And they were all young men, and they were exceedingly valiant for courage, and also for strength and activity; but behold, this was not all — they were men who were true at all times in whatsoever thing they were entrusted.

Alma 53:20

Lyman went into the department store with a twenty-dollar bill in his pocket. He was there to buy a new pair of pants. He had felt that his old pair was good for another six months, but his wife had told him not to come home until he had bought a new pair. He tried on several pair and settled on the ones he wanted.

He paid for the pants and started to leave the store. As he went to put the change in his pocket, he realized that he had been given ten dollars too much. He immediately went back to the counter and told the clerk of his error. That's when Lyman's troubles began. Lyman learned the hard way that it is not always easy to be honest.

The clerk's supervisor was standing a few feet away, which may have been the reason for the clerk's reaction. At any rate, the clerk said that he did not make mistakes and that he was positive that he had given the right change. Lyman explained to him that he had only had a twenty-dollar bill when he came in, and now he had a pair of pants and fifteen dollars.

The clerk again refused to accept the ten-dollar bill and told Lyman that he must have had a ten-dollar bill in his pocket that he was not aware of. For most people, this would have been a good enough reason for keeping the ten-dollar bill and leaving the store. Many people would have even rejoiced that they had done their best and were now ten dollars richer.

Lyman, however, was not like most people. He had made a commitment to himself and to the Lord that he would try to be totally honest. Lyman tried to argue one more time with the clerk and finally said, "This ten dollars is not mine and I will not take it. You can put it in your till or put it in your pocket, but you cannot make me dishonest for ten dollars." He laid the ten-dollar bill on the counter and walked out of the store. He could then go home because he had purchased a new pair of pants as his wife had directed.

Teaching Ideas and Related Scriptures

Honesty: This story teaches an attitude that all of us could benefit from. Lyman would not accept any excuse to be dishonest and was totally committed to the principle of honesty. He believed that God sets the principle of honesty, not a clerk in a store. A very effective way of teaching with this story would be to stop reading or telling it after you had related the clerk's second refusal to accept the money and then to ask some questions such as: "What would you do?" "Why?" "What would Heavenly Father like you to do?" "What do you think Lyman did?" Then you could finish the story and discuss the principle of honesty.

Alma 27:27. "And they were among the people of Nephi, and also numbered among the people who were of the church of God. And they were also distinguished for their zeal towards God, and also towards men; for they were perfectly honest and upright in all things; and they were firm in the faith of Christ, even unto the end." (*See also* Alma 53:20; D&C 51:9; D&C 97:8.)

Don't Just
Sit There

Yea, behold, I will tell you in your mind and in your heart, by the Holy Ghost, which shall come upon you and which shall dwell in your heart.

D&C 8:2

When John Squires's wife died, leaving him with several motherless children, Brigham Young advised him to marry a strong young woman to help raise his children. John asked a nineteen-year-old young woman named Emily to marry him. Her confidence in Brigham Young must have been as great as his because she accepted the proposal even though they had only met a few times. The following experience is a good example of the great faith they had that President Young was a man of God.

Their first baby was critically ill. In fact, she was dying, when a call came to John Squires from President Young to leave immediately to accompany him on a trip to southern Utah. John sent back word of the conditions at his home, and Brigham Young's company went on without him. When they reached the "Point of the Mountain" between Salt Lake City and Provo, Brigham Young was still thinking about John and Emily and their sick baby. He sent word to John and promised him and Emily that if John would come and join him their baby would be made whole. Trusting implicitly in this promise, John left his wife and sick baby and joined President Young.

Emily was still just a young mother and was inexperienced in taking care of children, especially those that were sick. Before John left, all she had done was sit and cry, holding the sick baby. John was older and more experienced with children but had not known what to do for the baby either. No medical aid was available, so when priesthood administrations did not bring immediate results, they felt the child would die.

11

John had no sooner left to do what President Young had asked him to do than this thought came to Emily: "Don't just sit here doing nothing and let your baby die!" A method of treatment flashed into her mind as clearly as if she had seen someone do it before. She gathered some stones and put them in the hot coals in the fireplace. She then sat with a shawl around her and the baby on her lap and placed a bucket of water at her feet. She would drop a hot stone in the bucket of water, causing steam to rush up the inside of the shawl. As soon as the steam ceased, she would drop another hot stone into the bucket. In this way Emily steamed the baby until her fever broke and she fell asleep, breathing naturally. The baby grew to womanhood, and John and Emily always felt that her life was a gift from God for their faith in a promise made by a prophet of the Lord.

Teaching Ideas and Related Scriptures

Faith: This story is a perfect example of faith. Without great faith, John could never have left and Emily could never have let him go. Because they had the faith to respond to the prophet, they received the help they needed through the Holy Ghost.

2 Nephi 26:13. "And that he manifesteth himself unto all those who believe in him, by the power of the Holy Ghost; yea, unto every nation, kindred, tongue, and people, working mighty miracles, signs, and wonders, among the children of men according to their faith." (*See also* Proverbs 3:5–6; 1 Nephi 7:12; Alma 57:26; Helaman 12:1.)

Following Counsel of Leaders: When we follow our leaders' counsel, we put ourselves in a position to receive the Lord's help. When a prophet gives us direction or makes us a promise, he speaks for the Lord and it is as if the Lord had spoken.

D&C 21:5–6. "For his word ye shall receive, as if from mine own mouth, in all patience and faith.

"For by doing these things the gates of hell shall not prevail against you; yea, and the Lord God will disperse the powers of darkness from before you, and cause the heavens to shake for your good, and his name's glory." (*See also* D&C 1:38; D&C 84:36.)

Inspiration: Two ways the Holy Ghost speaks to us are to our minds and to our hearts. He speaks to our minds by giving us ideas and thoughts, such as he did to Emily in this story. When he speaks to our hearts, he gives us feelings that can guide us in our lives.

D&C 8:2–3. "Yea, behold, I will tell you in your mind and in your heart, by the Holy Ghost, which shall come upon you and which shall dwell in your heart.

"Now, behold, this is the spirit of revelation." (*See also* D&C 11:13; D&C 39:6.)

Latter-day Prophets; Brigham Young: Modern-day prophets are as inspired as those in olden times. They are also sensitive, as is taught by the fact that President Young continued to think about the family and the baby and wanted to help them if he could. When a prophet, past or present, makes a promise, it will come to pass if the conditions of the promise are met.

D&C 1:38. "What I the Lord have spoken, I have spoken, and I excuse not myself; and though the heavens and the earth pass away, my word shall not pass away, but shall all be fulfilled, whether by mine own voice or by the voice of my servants, it is the same." (*See also* D&C 21:5–6; D&C 68:3–4.)

Obedience: In this story, it is easy to see the correlation between obedience and receiving a promised blessing, but God says that all obedience brings blessings.

D&C 130:20–21. "There is a law, irrevocably decreed in heaven before the foundations of this world, upon which all blessings are predicated—

"And when we obtain any blessing from God, it is by obedience to that law upon which it is predicated." (*See also* Deuteronomy 6:24–25; Deuteronomy 7:12–15; D&C 59:23.)

Who Is the Man with the Hair?

But the Lord said unto Samuel, Look not on his countenance, or on the height of his stature; because I have refused him: for the Lord seeth not as man seeth; for man looketh on the outward appearance, but the Lord looketh on the heart.

1 Samuel 16:7

As sacrament meeting started in one of the Brigham Young University student wards, everyone in the congregation was excited and curious. The bishopric had been changed the previous week, but the new second counselor had not been presented because he had been out of town; he was to be presented this week instead.

As people had looked around during the earlier "block" meetings for who it might be, many had noticed a bearded fellow that did not look like he belonged. The dress standards at Brigham Young University are strict, and this man broke all of the hair standards with his full beard, very long hair, and thick mustache.

A few of the students assumed he must be a visitor accompanying one of the students. A few other students thought that this was their chance to do some missionary work. Most of the students, however, made snide remarks about the stranger and had nothing to do with him. The poor guy was given all kinds of looks during the course of the morning, and almost everyone made a judgment about him in some way or another.

You can imagine the surprise of the ward members when, during sacrament meeting, this "visitor" was called up to the front to be presented and sustained as the new second counselor to the bishop.

"It was very interesting," the bishop began, "as I sat through priesthood meeting and Sunday School this morning and watched you as you noticed this hairy young man sitting among us. I wondered what some of you were thinking and didn't need to wonder about others as they volunteered little comments here and there.''

The bishop then introduced the man and told the members that he had special permission to wear his beard, mustache, and long hair. He was playing the part of John the Baptist in a new Church film.

The stake president then stood and asked the members of the ward to sustain their new second counselor. A great lesson on judging others had been learned, and all raised their hands to the square.

Teaching Ideas and Related Scriptures

Unrighteously Judging Others: This is a pretty straightforward story for teaching the problem of unrighteously judging others. When telling the story, you might consider leaving off the beginning about a bishopric change and then stop the story halfway through. You could ask those whom you are teaching why this man might have attended this Brigham Young University ward even though he was apparently violating Brigham Young University grooming standards. You could then ask how the students should react to the man. Then finish the story.

John 7:24. "Judge not according to the appearance, but judge righteous judgment." (*See also* 1 Samuel 16:7; Matthew 7:1-2; Moroni 7:18.)

That Is the Worst Lesson I've Ever Heard

> And no one can assist in this work except he shall be humble and full of love, having faith, hope, and charity, being temperate in all things, whatsoever shall be entrusted to his care.
>
> *D&C 12:8*

The new missionary district leader could not believe what he was hearing. He was listening to Elder Parker, who had been out for almost two years, stumble his way through the first discussion. Any missionary of worth who had been out three weeks or longer knew the first discussion, but Elder Parker didn't. The early morning study session came to a close and Elder Parker left with his companion.

The new district leader turned to his companion, shook his head and said, "That's the worst first discussion I have ever heard. Isn't Elder Parker dedicated enough to learn the discussions?" His companion was surprised that he did not know the discussion; he had always felt that Elder Parker was an excellent missionary.

The next day was their first district meeting of the month, and each of the companionships was to come prepared to share its goals for the new month. It was not an easy mission to baptize in, and the baptism goal of each companionship ranged from three to five people. Then it was Elder Parker's turn to share his baptism goal for the month. When he said that they were planning on baptizing twenty people that month, the district leader almost laughed out loud. He thought to himself, *Elder Parker doesn't even know the first discussion but is going to baptize twenty people. This I have to see.*

The next week when the missionaries met, the only Elders who had baptized were Elder Parker and his companion. They had baptized five people. The district leader wanted to see how Elder Parker could baptize so many despite his not knowing the discussions, so he asked to go with Elder Parker the next time he was going to teach a first discussion.

The next day, the district leader received a phone call and was invited to go with Elder Parker the following morning to help him teach the first discussion to an interested family. In those days, the discussions were memorized and given almost word for word. Missionaries would take turns, each giving a few paragraphs and shifting back and forth so it seemed like an informal discussion. Elder Parker started the discussion and completely murdered the first part. The district leader took his turn and tried to bring some order back to the flow of the discussion. It was then Elder Parker's turn again—he completely skipped several key paragraphs. By the end of the lesson, the district leader was totally disoriented and confused. He felt that the family probably felt the same way.

When the discussion was over, Elder Parker leaned forward and put his hand on the arm of the family's father. He then looked him straight in the eyes, told him how much he loved him and his family, and bore one of the most humble and powerful testimonies that the district leader had ever heard. By the time he finished, every member of the family, including the father, and both Elders had tears running down their cheeks. Next Elder Parker taught the father how to pray, and they all knelt down while the father prayed that they might receive testimonies of their own and thanked Heavenly Father for the great love that he felt. Two weeks later the whole family was baptized.

As they were driving away from the discussion, Elder Parker apologized to the district leader. He told him that he felt very bad that he did not know the discussions better. He said that he had always had a problem with memorization. He said that he got up at five-thirty instead of six o'clock every morning and spent two hours on the discussions but could never remember them well when it came time to teach them. He explained that he knelt in prayer before teaching each family and talked with Heavenly Father about his problem. He would ask Heavenly Father to bless him so that when he bore his testimony the

18

people would feel his love and the Spirit and know that they were being taught the truth.

Humbled, the district leader spent the rest of the day pondering what he had learned about teaching the gospel. For the first time he realized that it was not discussions but love and the Spirit that converted people to the gospel. The district leader never taught the gospel the same way again.

Teaching Ideas and Related Scriptures

Humility: Elder Parker demonstrated the importance that humility plays in having the Lord's help when we are trying to help others.

D&C 112:10. "Be thou humble; and the Lord thy God shall lead thee by the hand, and give thee answer to thy prayers." (*See also* Matthew 20:25-28; Helaman 3:35; D&C 12:8; D&C 38:41.)

Judging Others: The district leader learned a lesson about judging others without the Spirit or even all of the facts. He thought that the Elder was lazy when actually he was working harder than the district leader.

Moroni 7:18. "And now, my brethren, seeing that ye know the light by which ye may judge, which light is the light of Christ, see that ye do not judge wrongfully; for with that same judgment which ye judge ye shall also be judged." (*See also* 1 Samuel 16:7; Matthew 7:1-2; Romans 8:27; James 2:13.)

Love: The story demonstrates the importance that love plays when teaching the gospel.

D&C 12:8. "And no one can assist in this work except he shall be humble and full of love, having faith, hope, and charity, being temperate in all things, whatsoever shall be entrusted to his care." (*See also* John 13:34-35; Galatians 5:13-14; 1 John 4:20-21; Moroni 7:48.)

Missionary Work: This story can be used as a good example of the kind of missionary work that changes lives—missionary work done with love and the Spirit.

D&C 42:14. "And the Spirit shall be given unto you by the prayer of faith; and if ye receive not the Spirit ye shall not teach." (*See also* Galatians 5:13–14; D&C 12:8; D&C 50:13–14; D&C 50:17–18.)

Teaching: This is also an excellent story to use when teaching teachers how to teach. It stresses the importance of teaching with love and with the Spirit.

D&C 50:13–14. "Wherefore, I the Lord ask you this question —unto what were ye ordained?

"To preach my gospel by the Spirit, even the Comforter which was sent forth to teach the truth." (*See also* D&C 12:8; D&C 42:14; D&C 50:17–18.)

It Changed My Life

And now, it has hitherto been wisdom in God that these things should be preserved; for behold, they have enlarged the memory of this people, yea, and convinced many of the error of their ways, and brought them to the knowledge of their God unto the salvation of their souls.

Alma 37:8

Elder Paskett and his companion were assigned to a little Mexican city on the border of Sonara and Arizona. In fact, the international border divided the city. The Elders soon became aware that they had bitter opposition from the town constable. He had a strong influence on town members and at times made their lives very difficult. In spite of this, however, he allowed the Elders to teach his wife the gospel. Apparently he loved his wife very much and gave in to her requests to hear the gospel. He would not, however, allow the Elders to come on his property. He compromised by permitting them to teach his wife over the low, rock wall surrounding his yard. She would come from the house and approach the wall. The Elders would then come up to the wall from the street, put their books on its flat top, and teach her the gospel.

One evening, a little Mexican boy came to the door of the Elders' apartment with a written message for them. The note was from the constable and requested their company at his home the following evening if it was convenient for them. They sent a note back by the little boy telling him that it would be a pleasure to accept his invitation.

The following evening, as the Elders approached the gate of their intended host, he came out of the gate to greet them. As they were visiting with him, he asked, "Perhaps you're wondering why I've had a change of heart and invited you to dinner?"

The missionaries assured him that they were somewhat curious. He then explained, "I was home alone a portion of one afternoon. I knew that there was no one around to see me, so I took a look at my wife's Book of Mormon. I opened it at random and started to read. What I read profoundly affected me. I changed my entire concept and outlook on life.''

He then requested a Book of Mormon in English. His wife's book was in Spanish. He explained that he could read Spanish but understood English better. He then told the missionaries that if they wanted to hold street meetings, they shouldn't hold them on the sidewalk. He said that the sidewalk was too narrow and uncomfortable. He told them to instead go to the town plaza and talk from the bandstand. He even suggested that they arrange the benches around the bandstand in any order that they desired. He then promised that he would be there to see that no one bothered them.

He was true to his word. He came often with his wife and brought his married daughter several times. Because of experiences like these, Elder Paskett still refers to Mexico as Book of Mormon country.

Teaching Ideas and Related Scriptures

Book of Mormon: The Book of Mormon is the greatest single missionary tool of the Church. The immediate effect it can have on people is illustrated in this story.

Alma 37:8. ''And now, it has hitherto been wisdom in God that these things should be preserved; for behold, they have enlarged the memory of this people, yea, and convinced many of the error of their ways, and brought them to the knowledge of their God unto the salvation of their souls.''

Missionary Work: This story demonstrates the great power of God's word in getting people to change their lives and do that which is right.

Alma 31:5. ''And now, as the preaching of the word had a great tendency to lead the people to do that which was just — yea, it had had more powerful effect upon the minds of the people than the sword, or anything else, which had happened unto them — therefore Alma thought it was expedient that they should try the virtue of the word of God.'' (See also 2 Nephi 31:20; 2 Nephi 32:3; Helaman 3:29-30.)

I'm a Good Mormon

And he answering said, Thou shalt love the Lord thy God with all thy heart, and with all thy soul, and with all thy strength, and with all thy mind; and thy neighbour as thyself.

Luke 10:27

As the two teenage boys sauntered through the restaurant parking lot, one of them spotted a two-foot piece of pipe laying on the blacktop by the fence. He picked it up and suggested to the other boy that they use it to break out the windshields of the cars that were parked there. The second boy thought this was a good idea, so they took turns swinging the pipe against the car windshields. It only took them a few minutes to shatter over fifty windshields. They then threw the pipe into the weeds and hurried on down the street. The first few people to finish their meals and come out of the restaurant could not believe the damage that had been done.

The police were called and began looking for eyewitnesses. No one in the restaurant had seen or heard anything out of the ordinary. Their last hope was a house that was on the property next to the restaurant. Two policemen went up the steps and knocked on the door. A middle-aged woman opened the door, and the police asked if they could come in for a moment. They then asked the woman if she had seen anything out of the ordinary happen in the parking lot next door.

The woman hesitated for a moment, and then she told how she had seen two boys pick up a pipe and break out all of the car windshields in the parking lot. The police could not understand why she had not said or done anything and asked her why she had not stepped outside and yelled or at least called the police. Her answer is a classic. She said that she was a good Mormon and did not want to get involved because her name would then be on police records.

The policemen, who were also Latter-day Saints were completely shocked by her answer. To them, being a good Latter-day Saint included caring enough about others to get involved even if it was inconvenient or, in some cases, risky.

Teaching Ideas and Related Scriptures

Love: Love is demonstrated by doing, not just talking. A real concern for others moves us to act in their behalf. Sometimes it may even be risky or costly as we show our love by becoming involved and helping those around us.

D&C 82:19. "Every man seeking the interest of his neighbor, and doing all things with an eye single to the glory of God." (*See also* Matthew 7:12; Luke 10:25–37; Galatians 6:10; Mosiah 2:17.)

Parable of the good Samaritan: The purpose of the parable was to show who our neighbor is and how to show love to them. The Samaritan stopped and helped at risk and cost to himself. The parable teaches that everyone, even strangers, are our neighbors. (*See* Luke 10:25–37.)

She Rolled
Her Own

Elder Bridges and his companion had knocked on doors for six straight weeks without teaching anyone. That is why they were so surprised when the lady at the door, who called herself Dolly, cheerfully invited them to come in and tell her their message. She was a gray-haired grandma that just radiated warmth, kindness, and love.

The Elders decided to teach her the first discussion right there on the spot and set up the flannel board that missionaries used at that time. As they told her about Joseph Smith and the Restoration, she took out a sack of tobacco and a piece of paper and began to hand roll a cigarette. She was so good at it that, once the tobacco was in the paper, she could roll the cigarette with one hand. Elder Bridges was so fascinated with her dexterity that he almost forgot the lesson.

By the time the Elders were through discussing the First Vision, she had rolled and smoked three cigarettes. She then asked the Elders if they would like a cup of tea, which, of course, they had to refuse. She then invited them to come back for dinner, which, of course, they accepted.

Dinner turned out to be an experience that neither Elder has ever forgotten. She served them from huge pots on the stove with a very large ice cream scoop. The potatoes on each plate must have measured at least six inches high. Elders like to eat, but this was a task even for them. As they struggled through the gigantic plates of food and finally, with great effort, put it all away, she said, "I know how hungry growing boys are!" and leaped up, grabbed their plates and filled them the same way again. They looked at each other, grimaced, and attacked their second helping. By the time they were through eating, they felt very ill. They had never realized that food could seem so dangerous if taken in large amounts.

Dolly then proceeded to place in front of each one a huge plate with three desserts on it and told them to dive in. Both Elders knew that they had been given an impossible task and feel to this day that the Lord interceded on their behalf. At that very moment, a dog came into the backyard and started chasing Dolly's cat. As she ran out the back door to see what the racket was, the Elders looked at each other, sped to the sink, and scraped their desserts down the drain. They quickly ran some water to wash it down and hustled back to the table. When Dolly came back in the kitchen, they acted as if they were taking their last bite of dessert. When she indicated they had eaten it very quickly and probably wanted seconds, they finally, in unison, said, "No!"

They came back three days later and taught the second discussion. Once again, Dolly rolled and smoked her cigarettes all through the discussion. They became more and more concerned that she would never commit to live the Word of Wisdom and dreaded the day that they would teach the lesson.

However, soon that day arrived. As they set up the flannel board, she started on her first cigarette. They discussed the four things that members of the Church were asked to avoid and placed "tea," "coffee," "alcohol," and "tobacco" on the flannel board as they were discussed. Dolly continued to smoke throughout the discussion. When she was asked to identify the four things Heavenly Father did not want her to take into her body, she looked through the smoke curling up from her cigarette and read the four things that were on the flannel board. When she was asked if she would commit to live the Word of Wisdom, she changed the subject and refused to make a commitment. The Elders asked her to pray about it and left her with a cigarette still in her hand.

When they came back the next day, she sat them down and said, "Let me tell you a story." She had decided the night before that the Word of Wisdom was too hard to live and had rolled three cigarettes and placed them on her mantel. She did this because she was too shaky to roll her own in the mornings. She then went to bed and tried to go to sleep, but every time she closed her eyes all she could see were the word strips on the flannel board that said "no tea, coffee, alcohol, or tobacco." This went on for hours; finally, about two o'clock in the morning, she decided to kneel down and pray about the Word of Wisdom as the Elders had asked her to. As she asked Heavenly Father about the Word of Wisdom, a New Testament scripture came into her mind: "God so loved the world that he gave his only begotten Son." This good lady started to cry as God filled her heart with the love that he had for her. She then said to herself, "If God loves me this much and was willing to give up his Son for me, I can give up my cigarettes and tea for him."

When she finished this story, she told the Elders that she knew that the Word of Wisdom was God's will because he had answered her prayer. Three weeks later she became a member of the Church.

Teaching Ideas and Related Scriptures

Holy Ghost as a Source of Testimony in Missionary Work: This story exemplifies well that the Lord, not missionaries, converts people. Missionaries only teach and encourage. When the missionaries left for the night, Dolly was still smoking. When they came back the next morning, she had made a covenant with the Lord to never smoke again.

Alma 5:46. "Behold, I say unto you they are made known unto me by the Holy Spirit of God. Behold, I have fasted and prayed many days that I might know these things of myself. And now I do know of myself that they are true; for the Lord God hath made them manifest unto me by his Holy Spirit; and this is the spirit of revelation which is in me." (*See also* 2 Nephi 33:1; 3 Nephi 11:36; Moroni 10:4–5; D&C 50:13–14; D&C 50:21–22.)

Prayer: Prayer is absolutely vital in the process of gaining a testimony and living the gospel. Through prayer, not only can we gain confirmation of the truth but we can also receive the power we need to overcome temptations and keep our covenants. Without prayer, Dolly would still be rolling her own today.

Moroni 10:4-5. "And when ye shall receive these things, I would exhort you that ye would ask God, the Eternal Father, in the name of Christ, if these things are not true; and if ye shall ask with a sincere heart, with real intent, having faith in Christ, he will manifest the truth of it unto you, by the power of the Holy Ghost.

"And by the power of the Holy Ghost ye may know the truth of all things." (*See also* Jeremiah 29:13; 2 Nephi 32:8-9; Alma 5:46.)

Word of Wisdom: Dolly decided to live the Word of Wisdom because she loved God and felt his love for her. That is probably the best reason for us to live the Word of Wisdom also. Any physical blessings are really only secondary.

1 Corinthians 3:16-17. "Know ye not that ye are the temple of God, and that the Spirit of God dwelleth in you?

"If any man defile the temple of God, him shall God destroy; for the temple of God is holy, which temple ye are." (*See also* Daniel 1:8; D&C 49:18-21; D&C 59:20; D&C 89:1-21; D&C 93:35.)

Love of God: As Dolly felt God's love enter her heart and realized what God had done for her, she wanted to return that love through living an obedient life. If we consider the ways God has shown his love to us, we should desire to live better lives also.

John 3:16. "For God so loved the world, that he gave his only begotten Son, that whosoever believeth in him should not perish, but have everlasting life." (*See also* Romans 8:35; 1 Corinthians 2:9; 1 John 4:19; 2 Nephi 1:15; D&C 138:2-3.)

The Test

The smell of autumn was in the air as Marilee and her mother
drove to Provo, Utah, for the job interview. Marilee had received
a scholarship to Brigham Young University, but it just wasn't
enough. She still needed a job to pay for housing, food, and her
own personal needs. Coming from a large family has many ad-
vantages, but this was not one of them. The job was essential for
her college existence.

Marilee had been given a high recommendation by her previous employer and knew that she had a pretty good chance at the
position. Her only worry was that her previous manager had
honored her request to not work on the Sabbath. She didn't
know whether this manager would do the same.

She was told that she had the job and could start on Monday.
The manager, however, said that almost everyone who worked
there was LDS and she would be required to work one Sunday a
month. This became a very difficult decision for Marilee. She
understood the manager's point of view but had always placed
great value on Sabbath observance. She realized how many
young people were looking for work in Provo and knew it would
be difficult to find other employment.

After discussing the situation with her mother, she decided to
turn the job down. She just didn't feel good about working even
one Sunday a month.

Tears welled up in her eyes as they drove back to the Salt
Lake Valley where they lived. She realized she could not make

it through the school year without a job, and she had just given up a good one.

Marilee moved into her dorm, and school started the following week. A little over a month passed and she still had no job. One day she noticed an ad on one of the bulletin boards which read "Custodial job opening." She soon found why the job was open. The job consisted of cleaning offices and classrooms in the science building from 4:00 A.M. to 7:00 A.M. This meant getting up at 3:30 each morning and walking twenty minutes in the dark across the campus to work. She would then have one hour to dash back to her room, shower, and get ready for her 8:00 class.

Because of difficulty in keeping employees, the employer insisted that Marilee promise that she would work the entire semester. Walking across the dark campus in the middle of the night took more courage than she realized she had, but Marilee kept her word.

The last week of the semester, Marilee went to the employment office to see if there were any new job openings for the next semester. She noticed that there was a job open in one of the cafeterias on campus. The people in the employment office told her to call the cafeteria manager, but the Spirit directed her instead to the Missionary Training Center, which is on the Brigham Young University campus. When she got there, to her delight a job had just opened up that fit perfectly with her new winter semester schedule. She was hired on the spot. She didn't realize until later that the job she received was usually given to workers with seniority.

Marilee finished up the week at the science building in order to keep her word. She realized that she had been tested to see how strong she felt about Sabbath observance. She felt that her new job, with better working conditions and better pay, was a reward from Heavenly Father, and she felt very grateful. A few weeks later these feelings were confirmed in a priesthood blessing that she received. She was told in the blessing what she already felt in her heart—her new job was a gift from Heavenly Father for her love and devotion to him. She worked at the Missionary Training Center for two and a half years until she departed for her mission to Chile. Her job was waiting for her when she returned.

Teaching Ideas and Related Scriptures

Faith: It took faith for Marilee to turn down a job she really needed when she didn't know if she could find another one. Nevertheless she trusted that God would help her find a way to stay in school.

1 Nephi 3:7. "And it came to pass that I, Nephi, said unto my father: I will go and do the things which the Lord hath commanded, for I know that the Lord giveth no commandments unto the children of men, save he shall prepare a way for them that they may accomplish the thing which he commandeth them." (*See also* Hebrews 6:12–15; James 2:24; 1 Nephi 7:12.)

Obedience: God has promised us that when we obey any of his commandments, he will bless us. Some of the blessings are not as easy to see as the one in this story, but obedience always brings blessings into our lives.

D&C 130:20–21. "There is a law, irrevocably decreed in heaven before the foundations of this world, upon which all blessings are predicated—

"And when we obtain any blessing from God, it is by obedience to that law upon which it is predicated." (*See also* Deuteronomy 7:12–15; Isaiah 1:19; D&C 59:23.)

Sabbath: One of the promised blessings of keeping the Sabbath holy is temporal blessings from our Father in Heaven. Marilee's story is a good example of this promise being fulfilled. Of course, Sabbath observance brings many spiritual blessings as well.

D&C 59:9–10. "And that thou mayest more fully keep thyself unspotted from the world, thou shalt go to the house of prayer and offer up thy sacraments upon my holy day;

"For verily this is a day appointed unto you to rest from your labors, and to pay thy devotion unto the Most High." (*See also* Exodus 20:8–10; Exodus 31:13–17; Nehemiah 10:31; Nehemiah 13:15; Isaiah 56:2–7; D&C 59:9–24.)

I'll See You This Afternoon, Sister!

Now my brethren, we see that God is mindful of every people, whatsoever land they may be in; yea, he numbereth his people, and his bowels of mercy are over all the earth. Now this is my joy, and my great thanksgiving; yea, and I will give thanks unto my God forever. Amen.

Alma 26:37

Just five weeks after having open heart surgery, Betty began to feel and look as if she were pregnant. The doctor found a possible tumor instead and immediately checked her into the hospital. When they operated they found that cancer had spread throughout most of Betty's body. Because her heart stopped during the operation and because the cancer was so wide spread, they performed only minor surgery and closed Betty back up again.

When the doctors told Betty's husband that she had approximately six weeks to live, the news devastated him. They had done everything together and were each other's best friends. At that moment a huge feeling of emptiness filled his soul.

This experience with cancer caused Betty and her husband to draw closer to Heavenly Father than they had ever been before. They were so grateful that they felt no desire to curse or blame God and realized how much they needed his help and comfort.

Two weeks after Betty found out she had cancer, the Lord manifested his great love for her and her husband. They attended the October session of general conference on Temple Square in Salt Lake City. Following the morning session of conference, they went out behind the tabernacle to see if they could shake hands with President David O. McKay, who was then President of the Church. For some reason, no one was allowed to get close to the prophet that morning.

Somewhat disappointed, Betty and her husband left Temple Square and began to walk back to their car. As they were walking along the sidewalk, a car pulled up next to them in the street —it was President McKay. The prophet rolled down his window, looked directly at Betty, and said "I'll see you this afternoon, Sister!" He then rolled up his car window and drove away.

This really shocked Betty and her husband, and they couldn't figure out what was happening. They had planned to go home and watch the afternoon session of conference on television but this plan was quickly changed. Following the afternoon session, they again went around behind the tabernacle to see what would happen. They had no idea of what to expect.

As President McKay came out of the tabernacle, he looked around the crowd until he found Betty and then walked directly up to her. Taking her by the arm, he walked her away from the crowd and stopped between some of the tabernacle pillars where they could be alone. He then took her hand and talked to her for several minutes. He told her things that her soul needed to hear. He told her that she would be okay and not to worry anymore.

Betty was so filled with the Spirit that radiated from this great man that she became weak and began to shake. After President McKay left, her husband took her by the arm and helped her sit down on one of the benches. He kept asking her what President McKay had said, but it took several minutes before she could stop trembling and gain her composure enough to answer him.

The next week Betty and her husband went to California to visit relatives. This trip had originally been planned as a trip to say good-bye, but now they did not know what to think. They were not sure what President McKay meant when he told Betty that she would be all right. Because Betty was so weak, before going on the trip she received a beautiful blessing from her stake president.

While in California, they had the opportunity to do baptisms for the dead and to participate in several temple sessions. During one of these sessions they participated in a prayer that is offered in the temple. As the temple worker knelt at the altar and offered the prayer, he said that a woman was present who had traveled a great distance to be there. He mentioned that she had come with her family and had received a blessing from her priesthood leader before coming. Betty knew that he was talking about her. The temple worker then proceeded to repeat the blessing almost word for word that Betty had received from her stake president. As she heard the words of that special prayer, tears came to her eyes and peace and gratitude entered her heart.

This experience was very special for Betty, but especially meaningful to her husband. He realized for the first time just how important each of us is in the eyes of our Father in Heaven. He came to an understanding of how much God loved both of them and from that time forth desired to reciprocate that love.

When Betty returned to the doctor the following week, all signs of the cancer were completely gone! She had been totally healed.

This experience helped Betty come to the knowledge that the Lord knows each one of us personally. She learned that God does not just reveal programs and information for groups but gives revelations for specific individuals as well. In Betty's case, at least three priesthood leaders, including the prophet, were inspired by God in her behalf.

Teaching Ideas and Related Scriptures

Church Leaders; David O. McKay; Latter-day Prophets: God works through his divinely inspired servants to bless our lives. This is demonstrated as he used Betty's stake president, a temple worker, and even the President of the Church to bless her life.

1 Nephi 22:2. "And I, Nephi, said unto them: Behold they were manifest unto the prophet by the voice of the Spirit; for by the Spirit are all things made known unto the prophets, which shall come upon the children of men according to the flesh." (*See also* Amos 3:7; D&C 21:5-6.)

God Loves and Knows Each of Us: This story teaches clearly the important principle that God knows and loves us personally.

Alma 26:37. "Now my brethren, we see that God is mindful of every people, whatsoever land they may be in; yea, he numbereth his people, and his bowels of mercy are over all the earth. Now this is my joy, and my great thanksgiving; yea, and I will give thanks unto my God forever. Amen." (*See also* 1 Nephi 22:25; 2 Nephi 1:15.)

Divine Guidance: When we have troubles in our lives, we can either curse and blame God or do as Betty and her husband and turn to God for divine help and comfort.

Proverbs 3:5–6. "Trust in the Lord with all thine heart; and lean not unto thine own understanding.

"In all thy ways acknowledge him, and he shall direct thy paths." (*See also* Isaiah 58:11.)

Miracles: As we exercise our faith, God can and will work miracles in our lives as he did for Betty.

Alma 57:26. "And now, their preservation was astonishing to our whole army, yea, that they should be spared while there was a thousand of our brethren who were slain. And we do justly ascribe it to the miraculous power of God, because of their exceeding faith in that which they had been taught to believe—that there was a just God, and whosoever did not doubt, that they should be preserved by his marvelous power." (*See also* Mormon 9:15–21; Moroni 7:37; D&C 35:8.)

Angels Will Attend Her

Yea, and it came to pass that the Lord our God did visit us with assurances that he would deliver us; yea, insomuch that he did speak peace to our souls, and did grant unto us great faith, and did cause us that we should hope for our deliverance in him.

Alma 58:11

Rhonda left three small children in her car for just a moment while she ran into the elementary school. When she returned, her three-year-old Sarah was gone. The other two children said that a man with long dark hair, a beard, and a mustache had pulled Sarah out through an open window.

Rhonda immediately called the police; they began their search, but it was too late. The man had disappeared. Rhonda's husband, Mark, joined Rhonda, and they spent the next several hours with the police and the FBI. Later that evening a press conference was held, and Rhonda and Mark made a public plea for their daughter's safe return.

The community gave its total support to Rhonda and Mark. Volunteer fasts were organized, and even small children joined in the fasting and prayer. Youth in the Church and in the community passed out flyers. People of all faiths joined in their support.

By the time Rhonda and Mark arrived home that first night, it was very late. The bishop and some ward members had fed and cared for their other children and put them to bed. They were finally by themselves. They had been thinking about a priesthood blessing all day because in the past these blessings had always given them new information. Mark was nervous about giving Rhonda a blessing, because he was so sad. He didn't know if his emotional state would interfere with his ability to feel and respond to the Spirit.

They knelt down together and prayed that Mark would know the words to say and that the Spirit of the Lord would guide him. As Mark began to give Rhonda the blessing, he recognized the Spirit of the Lord and was prompted to bless Rhonda that she was not to feel guilty. The Spirit indicated that the kidnapping was solely and completely the act of the man who had done it and that he would feel guilty for it. Mark could almost feel guilt and anguish going into the soul of the kidnapper for what he had done.

Mark promised Rhonda that she would be sustained, and both Rhonda and Mark received a firm confirmation that Sarah would be okay. They received the knowledge that Sarah had many more important things to do in this life and that there was no power that would be able to harm her. The Spirit told them that angels were attending and supporting her. When the blessing was finished, they just sat and cried. They knew she would be protected from the elements and would not suffer for food and water. They knew Sarah would come back to them and grow up in their home. They hugged each other and cried for a long time because they knew their daughter would be okay.

When they woke up the next morning, they had the feeling that they would get Sarah back on Friday, which was three days away. On Friday morning they looked at each other and said, "Well, today is the day. The trial is about over." Sarah was found about nine-thirty that morning. Hunters found her wandering in a desert wash about ten miles outside of town. She had a few scratches and bruises but that was the extent of her physical injuries.

Rhonda and Mark first saw Sarah again in the emergency room, where she shared with them what had happened to her. Sarah said that she had been dropped off in the desert and had felt really scared. Then she saw a little girl that looked like her younger sister playing in the desert. This girl was building a great big pile of rocks, and when the rocks would fall down, she would laugh and laugh. Whenever Sarah felt really scared again, she said, this girl would come back and play with the rocks until she was not afraid anymore. As Mark and Rhonda heard this, they knew that angels really had assisted their daughter.

Sarah said that no one told her but that she just knew what to do for the days and nights that she was alone. She stayed near some trees for two of the days and nights. When it rained Thursday night, she got under the trees and did not get wet. Mark and Rhonda had been home praying that if she was out in the elements she would somehow find shelter and stay dry. They had told the Lord that if he could part the Red Sea, he could part a few raindrops.

On Friday morning Sarah knew she was to leave the trees and begin to walk. She said she knew where to walk because there was a pathway to guide her. This pathway led her out of the desert and to the hunters who found her. All of the promises the Lord had made in the priesthood blessing had come to pass.

Teaching Ideas and Related Scriptures

Ministering Angels: This story demonstrates that angels are very much involved in helping us in this life.

Moroni 7:29. "And because he hath done this, my beloved brethren, have miracles ceased? Behold I say unto you, Nay; neither have angels ceased to minister unto the children of men." (See also D&C 103:20; D&C 109:22.)

Faith and Hope: Mark and Rhonda's hope and faith in the Lord shows that even in severe trials we can find comfort.

Alma 58:11. "Yea, and it came to pass that the Lord our God did visit us with assurances that he would deliver us; yea, insomuch that he did speak peace to our souls, and did grant unto us great faith, and did cause us that we should hope for our deliverance in him." (See also Ether 12:6.)

Miracles: This story is a good example of how, through faith, miracles are taking place in our day.

Moroni 7:37. "It is by faith that miracles are wrought; and it is by faith that angels appear and minister unto men; wherefore, if these things have ceased wo be unto the children of men, for it is because of unbelief, and all is vain." (See also Alma 57:26; Mormon 9:15–21.)

Priesthood Blessings: This story is a great example of how we can gain peace and comfort through priesthood blessings. It also demonstrates how priesthood blessings can be given in times of emotional stress and need, not just in times of physical sickness.

D&C 19:38. ''Pray always, and I will pour out my Spirit upon you, and great shall be your blessing—yea, even more than if you should obtain treasures of earth and corruptibleness to the extent thereof.'' (*See also* Isaiah 49:13; D&C 21:9.)

What Can I Do to Be Happy?

> He that findeth his life shall lose it: and he that loseth his life for my sake shall find it.
>
> *Matthew 10:39*

The family sat around the bed in the hospital room where their mother was dying. They had been told that she had only a few hours to live. Alan, who was the oldest child, looked around the room at the faces of his family. His father, who seemed to be under control, was sitting across from him. Alan knew that all of them loved his mother very much and wondered what they were thinking about. His own thoughts went back over her life and the great courage she had shown even though she had been bed-ridden and in constant pain for the last ten to fifteen years.

His mother's back had been broken in several places, and, because of complications from other problems, it would never heal. This meant that she had to be in bed in constant traction in order to lessen the pain as much as possible.

Alan remembered one day that his mother had been depressed and had asked him to come over and talk to her. She wanted to know what she could do so that she wouldn't be depressed. Even though she was in pain she wanted to be happy. Alan didn't know what to tell her, so he said that he would fast and pray about it and talk to her again the next Sunday.

The answer that Alan received shocked him, and he didn't know how he was going to tell his mother. When Sunday arrived, Alan sat down with his mother and told her that she was being too selfish and only thinking of herself. What she needed to do, if she was going to be happy, was to quit worrying about her problems and start helping other people. She asked Alan how she could help others when she was in bed twenty-four hours a day. Alan really didn't know the answer to that problem and told her that he had given her the solution but it was up to her to figure out how to do it.

Now Alan remembered how his mother had responded to the Lord's answer and had filled her life with service for others. Alan's father would bring her the ingredients and she would prepare meals lying flat on her back in bed. She put up fruit and Alan's dad cooked it. She called volunteer agencies and found things that she could do to help others. She called people daily that were lonely and needed cheering up. She made gifts and had her husband deliver them. She taught a Primary class in her living room, which was possible because she lived close to the chapel.

A few weeks after she started to serve others in this way, she grabbed Alan by the hand and thanked him with tears in her eyes for giving her the guidance she needed to be happy. She told him that, at first, she wondered how she could do what the Lord had indicated. She then exercised her faith and said to herself, "If the Lord said I could do it then I can do it," and she started looking for ways to serve. She told Alan how it had brought meaning and purpose back into her life.

Alan's thoughts drifted back to the present, and he felt the sweet spirit of peace and calm that was in the room. As he looked at his father, he remembered the great love and devotion that he had shown as he had worked many extra hours to make his wife more comfortable. He had built a traction bed in the living room so she would not have to stay in the bedroom all of the time. When that worked, he designed a portable traction bed so that she could spend time visiting and staying with the children, who were all adults by this time. He even ripped out the passenger seat in the car and built a traction bed in the car. When he went to the store or to the temple, he took his wife with him and she knitted in the car while he did the shopping or went through the temple.

Alan remembered how whirlpool baths seemed to lessen the pain for his mother and how his dad had made a whirlpool bath out of a large cattle trough because he could not afford to buy one.

Alan thought about what had happened as his dad had taken care of his beloved wife. Day by day, as he had demonstrated selfless, loving service, he had slowly but surely developed the attributes of kindness, patience, and charity. Alan realized that his father had become a celestial person through serving his wife. Alan knew that his mother would have voluntarily suffered all that she had gone through for this one blessing alone.

The whole family was interrupted in their thoughts as a nurse entered the room and checked on their mother. The nurse seemed surprised and told the family that she didn't seem any closer to death than she had been several hours before. Since Alan's dad had been up all night, and had not eaten for many hours, he decided to snatch a quick meal in the hospital cafeteria.

The rest of the family stepped into the hall and began to discuss the situation. A sister-in-law told about the recent death of her mother. She told how her mother had been expected to die at any moment and yet had lived for several days. She said that they had really wanted someone to be with her when she passed away so someone had stayed in the room twenty-four hours a day. One night, the person had to leave for just a minute and her mother passed away while she was alone. The sister-in-law told how she had read and heard things that indicated that some people love their families so much that they are afraid they will hurt their feelings so they hang on. Even though they want to go, they linger because they don't want family members to feel bad or to mourn.

As the family went back into the room, Alan thought about what had been said. Their mother had been unconscious for many hours, and he wondered if she knew they were there and didn't want to hurt them.

He stepped to the bed and took her hand in his. He told her how much each family member loved her and how his dad had come to realize that it would be better for her to leave. He talked with her, shared their love, and said good-bye. A minute or two after he sat down, she took her last breath. His dad returned to the room just in time to see his wife leave this life.

Alan, being the oldest child, was then asked to represent the family in prayer. As the members of the family knelt around the bed, Alan understood for the first time just how wonderful the resurrection would be. He could not remember the last time he had seen his mother walking, yet she would walk again. He could not remember seeing her without her being in pain, yet she would receive a perfect, painless body. As he began to pray, he prayed not in sorrow or grief but in gratitude to Jesus for the Atonement and the Resurrection. The Holy Ghost brought into the heart of each one present the knowledge and assurance that their mother was alive and without pain in a much more beautiful place than this earth.

Even today Alan sometimes misses his mother, but he would not bring her back for anything but a short visit. He is so grateful that she is where she is; his goal is now to so live that he can be with her again.

Teaching Ideas and Related Scriptures

Adversity: In dealing with and overcoming adversity, we can develop qualities that will help us to become more Christlike. (*See* Revelation 2:10; Alma 26:27.)

Atonement and Resurrection: The Resurrection is a great blessing. Furthermore, the Atonement has rendered death without power.

Mosiah 16:8. "But there is a resurrection, therefore the grave hath no victory, and the sting of death is swallowed up in Christ." (*See also* Isaiah 25:8; D&C 42:46.)

Death: This would be an excellent story for teaching correct attitudes toward the death of a loved one; we can be comforted with the loss of family members and friends.

D&C 42:46. "And it shall come to pass that those that die in me shall not taste of death, for it shall be sweet unto them." (*See also* Isaiah 25:8; Mosiah 16:8.)

Service: The importance of service in overcoming depression and unhappiness and in becoming more like God is very well demonstrated by Alan's mother and father.

Matthew 10:39. "He that findeth his life shall lose it: and he that loseth his life for my sake shall find it." (*See also* Revelation 2:10; Mosiah 2:17; Alma 26:27.)

The Wrong Turn

But I say unto you: Mine angels shall go up before you, and also my presence.

D&C 103:20

The Vietnam War unfortunately wasted many lives. Although he had many close brushes with death, Lynn was one of the lucky ones who got out with nothing worse than "jungle rot" and scarred memories. During his tour of duty in Vietnam, Lynn fought in several combat situations and witnessed the death of countless men. One of those combat missions became the turning point in his life—the one that made him believe in God.

One night Lynn's squad, which consisted of ten men, was sent out on a nighttime ambush. The location was to be three miles from the rest of the company. When soldiers are sent on an ambush, they have to go exactly where they are sent. If they make a mistake and end up at another spot, and if their movement is picked up anywhere else, they are considered to be the enemy. It is then likely that artillery will be dropped on them.

On that dark night Lynn was directly behind the point man, whose name was LeRoy. LeRoy was an excellent point man, and Lynn had never known LeRoy to make a mistake while leading the men. But on that particular night, Lynn saw LeRoy make a wrong turn and knew LeRoy was leading them in the wrong direction. He tried to quietly yell to LeRoy, but as Lynn tried to yell he could not speak. He then tried to reach out for LeRoy but could not move his arm. LeRoy only got fifteen to twenty feet in front of him, but for some reason Lynn could not catch him.

After walking at least one mile in the wrong direction, LeRoy stopped and fell to the ground. As Lynn and some of the other

45

men caught up with him, they told LeRoy that he had gone the wrong direction. LeRoy said he knew that, then he started to cry. He told the men that as he was walking along, the figure of a man appeared before him. LeRoy recognized the man—it was his brother, who had been killed in Vietnam a year earlier. LeRoy said that his brother had led them to that spot, where they would be safe. Lynn and some of the other men wondered if LeRoy was cracking up.

They quickly radioed back to the commanding officer and told him they were not where they were supposed to be and that they were lost. The C.O. told them to stay where they were. He said that as soon as it was light, he would take the rest of the company to the ambush site that the night squad was supposed to have gone to. The next morning, when the rest of the company of about eighty men walked into that site, they were ambushed by the enemy. The company lost the first three men that walked in, but there were enough other men in the company to drive the enemy back. If Lynn's squad, who only had ten men, had walked to that site the night before, they would have all been killed. The ten men would not have been enough to drive the enemy back. Lynn now knew that LeRoy had not been crazy, but that LeRoy's brother had genuinely led them away from death the night before.

Lynn has wondered many times since that special night whether he was the person the Lord was protecting or if it was someone else in his squad. That night became a turning point in Lynn's life. He realized that there really was a God looking after them. Since returning home, Lynn has been sealed in the temple to his wife and children and has been active in the Church.

Teaching Ideas and Related Scriptures

Ministering Angels: Angels are sometimes sent to protect us from physical adversity and spiritual ruin. These angels may include deceased loved ones who are very concerned about our earthly welfare (see *Gospel Doctrine* [Salt Lake City: Deseret Book Co., 1970], pp. 435–36).

D&C 103:20. "But I say unto you: Mine angels shall go up before you, and also my presence." (*See also* Daniel 3:28; Acts 5:18–20; 1 Nephi 3:29; Moroni 7:29–30; D&C 109:22.)

We'll Pray
A Lot

Search diligently, pray always, and be believing, and all things shall work together for your good, if ye walk uprightly and remember the covenant wherewith ye have covenanted one with another.

D&C 90:24

Allan was the elders quorum president in his ward. He and his counselors had worked very hard to establish a close-knit and caring elders quorum. Just when things seemed to be going smoothly, Allan woke up one morning and discovered that he had lost his voice during the night. He thought it would just be a temporary thing, but it didn't come back.

He finally went to see the doctor, who said that Allan had a growth called a polyp that was pressing against his voice box. He further explained that it usually happened to people who did a lot of singing or a lot of talking. Allan later joked that those who had heard him sing knew that it came from a lot of talking. He was truly sorry that he talked so much when he found out that he would need an operation to remove the growth before he could talk again.

While he was waiting for the operation, Allan used a slate to communicate with others. He used a child's plastic slate that he could write on with a wooden pencil. He could then pull up the plastic and erase what he had written. Allan took it with him every place. By using this he was able to continue visiting the elders in their homes. When he would write something on the slate, many people would grab the slate and want to write something back. They thought that because he could not talk, he could not hear either.

As Allan continued to direct the elders quorum with the help of the slate, the Lord richly blessed the presidency. As they visited families, he would begin to write what he wanted to say on his slate. Before he could get his thoughts down in writing, one of his counselors would know exactly what he was going to write and say it to the family they were visiting. This happened time and time again, family after family.

One afternoon, while Allan was still waiting for his operation, his wife, Betty, received a phone call from a relative in Colorado informing her that Allan's nephew had been killed in a mine explosion. This came as a tremendous shock because he was such a young man and left a family with small children.

The family wanted to know if Allan and Betty could come to the funeral. Betty assured them that they would be able to attend. She could not talk to Allan over the phone so she told him about it when he got home from work. After learning of the tragedy, he agreed with Betty that they needed to go and give their support.

When they arrived the afternoon before the funeral, they were surprised to find out that the printed program had Allan listed as the only speaker at the funeral. Allan hadn't spoken for days, and the doctor had told him that he would not be able to speak until after the operation. He didn't know what to do.

As he tried to sort out his feelings, he realized that he was the only active Church member in his family. He then understood why they had chosen him to speak at the funeral. They were depending on him to give needed comfort and understanding to his nephew's wife and family.

Allan turned to Betty in desperation and wrote, ''Betty, what are we going to do?''

She answered that they would do the only thing that they could do. They would pray a lot during the night and rely on the Lord. Before they went to bed that night, they knelt at the foot of their motel bed and poured out their hearts to their Heavenly Father. Their desires were for their nephew's family and that somehow they would be able to give them the comfort and help that they needed.

When they woke up the next morning, Allan's voice was back. He was able to speak with the guidance of the Holy Ghost and explain the beautiful gospel plan. This seemed to bring great comfort to his nephew's family and friends.

Following the funeral, many family members asked numerous gospel questions about things that Allan had read about but could not remember. As he tried to answer these questions, the Spirit brought back the answers to his memory and he was able to further teach the gospel to his family.

After this family discussion, his voice left him and he could not speak again until after the operation. This has been a testimony to Allan of how much the Lord loves all of us and wants to give us comfort and hope in our times of distress.

Teaching Ideas and Related Scriptures

Dedication: Even though it seemed as if Allan had a good excuse for not doing his work as an elders quorum president and speaking at the funeral of his nephew, he did not give up.

D&C 90:24. "Search diligently, pray always, and be believing, and all things shall work together for your good, if ye walk uprightly and remember the covenant wherewith ye have covenanted one with another." (*See also* Matthew 6:33; 1 Nephi 3:15; Helaman 10:4.)

Faith: In their hour of need, Allan and Betty passed their test of faith by turning to the Lord, knowing he would help them accomplish the things that they needed to do.

1 Nephi 3:7. "And it came to pass that I, Nephi, said unto my father: I will go and do the things which the Lord hath commanded, for I know that the Lord giveth no commandments unto the children of men, save he shall prepare a way for them that they may accomplish the thing which he commandeth them." (*See also* Matthew 21:21-22; 1 Nephi 7:12; Ether 12:6, 12.)

Miracles: If we have faith and turn to God, he can perform miracles in all of our lives, as he did for Allan and Betty.

D&C 35:8. "For I am God, and mine arm is not shortened; and I will show miracles, signs, and wonders, unto all those who believe on my name." (*See also* 2 Nephi 26:13; Mormon 9:15-21.)

Prayer: God hears and answers our prayers if we will but turn to him in humility and trust.

D&C 112:10. "Be thou humble; and the Lord thy God shall lead thee by the hand, and give thee answer to thy prayers." (*See also* Matthew 7:7-8; 3 Nephi 18:20.)

Let's Be Kind

Ye are the light of the world. A city that is set on an hill cannot be hid.

Matthew 5:14

Brett and Frank worked for a roofing company. They were really enjoying the job they were on because of the lady that lived in the house they were working on. She was an older lady and a very kind person. She spent a lot of time watching them work or talking to them from the lawn.

After she had visited with them for a while, she told them that when they were finished she had some coffee and cookies for them. She then hustled into her house to get things ready.

Both Brett and Frank were Mormons, so they discussed what they should do about the coffee. Brett told Frank that they could not drink the coffee. Frank pointed out that the lady was so nice and seemed so happy to have someone to talk to that it would be wrong to hurt her feelings by refusing her offer. Frank insisted that one cup of coffee was not as important as being kind to the lady. Brett decided maybe he was right; this was a good reason for drinking the coffee.

When they had finished on the roof and put their tools away, they knocked on the back door. The kind lady opened the door and ushered them into her kitchen. She had three place mats set with a huge plate of cookies on two of them and a cup of coffee by each place mat.

When they saw how much trouble she had gone to, they were glad that they had decided not to hurt her feelings by refusing the coffee. They visited together and thoroughly enjoyed themselves as they drank their coffee and ate the cookies. The coffee didn't taste that good but the cookies were delicious.

When they had finished their coffee and cookies, the lady said, "You're Mormons, aren't you?"

The room became very quiet and finally Brett and Frank nodded their heads that they were. The lady then said something that Brett and Frank have not forgotten even though this happened over twenty years ago. She said, "Just as I thought. I've never seen a Mormon yet that lives his religion."

As Brett went home that day, he promised himself and Heavenly Father that he would never again make the mistake of breaking the Word of Wisdom out of fear for what someone may think. That was the last cup of coffee that Brett ever had. He would have given anything not to have had that one. He has often wondered how it would have felt to have her say, "I'm really surprised that you refused a cup of coffee. I realize now that there are Mormons who live their religion."

Teaching Ideas and Related Scriptures

Example: If Frank and Brett had done the right thing, their good example may have set the lady on her way to conversion instead of reinforcing her negative impression of the Church.

Matthew 5:14. "Ye are the light of the world. A city that is set on an hill cannot be hid." (*See also* Philippians 2:15; Jacob 2:35; Alma 4:10.)

Word of Wisdom: Many people say that just one cup of coffee won't hurt, but this story illustrates otherwise. One cup always hurts us, spiritually as well as physically.

D&C 89:18-19. "And all saints who remember to keep and do these sayings, walking in obedience to the commandments, shall receive health in their navel and marrow to their bones;

"And shall find wisdom and great treasures of knowledge, even hidden treasures." (*See also* 1 Corinthians 3:16–17; D&C 89:1-21; D&C 93:35.)

No Little Limbs Made Whole

He that handleth a matter wisely shall find good: and whoso trusteth in the Lord, happy is he.

Proverbs 16:20

Forty years ago, Margaret stood outside a school for the severely handicapped and listened to a lecture that included statistics on the incidence of birth defects and other abnormalities in the population. Her instructor told her and her classmates that some of them would have a child born with either a mental or physical abnormality. As she stood in the sunshine with a blue sky over her head, she looked at her fellow students and thought, "Well, maybe it will happen to some of them, but it's not going to happen to me."

But it did happen to her—and not just once. Of the four children born to Margaret and her husband, Bud, three had physical problems, each problem totally unrelated to the others.

They had been married just over two years when their first child was born. The pregnancy was going well for them, and the gloomy predictions of the social worker had been forgotten. Then the baby was born malformed, missing parts of her arms and legs. It was a terrible shock for a young couple expecting to gain everything life had to offer.

On that devastating day of their baby's birth, Margaret and Bud could not see into the future or foresee the blessings that would come to them because of the special children that would be born into their family. They only knew that life as they had known it was changed for them forever.

They were advised by everyone not to take their baby home but rather to put her in a nursing facility where she could receive adequate care. Margaret's sister kindly took the baby directly from the hospital to the nursing facility, and Margaret and Bud went home to the empty crib and unopened gifts of baby clothes and toys. They had crossed over into that lonely no man's island inhabited by those who are known to most only as "statistics."

But they felt that they wanted more children and were overjoyed, although apprehensive, to learn that a second child was on the way. They received many reassurances that their first baby was a one in ten thousand occurrence, and their doctor said that it would never happen again.

"You've had your share," was the opinion of friends and family members. Indeed, X rays showed this expectant baby with all of its limbs complete.

After a few months, in spite of what others said, they decided to bring their first child, also named Margaret, home from the nursing facility to stay. They, along with everyone else, waited eagerly for their second child.

When Bill Ray was born, they counted his fingers and toes and rejoiced. But he was thin and had trouble gaining weight. On top of that, he seemed prey to respiratory infections and was often down in bed with bronchitis or pneumonia.

When Bill Ray was two years old, he was diagnosed as having cystic fibrosis, a disease which affects the lungs and pancreas. At that time the average life expectancy for such a child was only two years.

This would be enough bad luck and sorrow to stop most parents from having any more children, but not Margaret and Bud. Before Margaret and Bill Ray celebrated their second and third birthdays, Margaret and Bud had a new baby girl who was born strong and healthy. Robin has since become the mother of their six grandchildren.

But their heartache was not over yet. When Robin was seven years old, Margaret became pregnant again. She was thirty-five years old and had not anticipated more children—not with the responsibilities of caring for two handicapped children and a lively second-grader.

Although it was a difficult pregnancy and birth, they had a beautiful baby boy, big and healthy looking. But he was missing a little valve in his bronchial tubes. He could breath in, but without the valve, he could not breath out.

He lived eight days, and Margaret was able to hold him only once.

Many couples, with the adversity that Margaret and Bud had to face might have become bitter or unhappy or even have turned against God. Margaret and Bud reacted in just the opposite way.

When they brought their first baby, Margaret, home from the nursing facility, they really didn't know what to do for her except to love her. She responded to their love and care and defied all medical prognostications by sitting when the doctors said she would not and by walking when they said she could not. She walked first by pushing a little rocking chair in front of her. She then used a walker made for her by her father. Finally she learned to walk using homemade crutches about three feet long that Bud especially designed for her. Even today, she still uses these crutches and has learned to go everywhere alone.

With the encouragement of family and friends, and a will that did not know the word *can't*, Margaret attended and finished all twelve grades of school. In spite of being told it was impossible and having to fight for admittance, she earned a degree from Brigham Young University. She then shocked everyone by saying she was going on a mission and, once again, overcame everyone's doubts by serving a successful mission in Texas.

Today she has her own job and apartment and drives her own redesigned car. She travels a great deal telling her story of faith and courage in sacrament meetings, firesides, seminars, and seminaries. She has brought great joy into the lives of her family members and friends.

Bill Ray was also a fighter. Margaret and Bud were stunned but determined when they found out he had cystic fibrosis; they began a battle to keep him alive that lasted twenty-eight years. They were supported by family members, friends, doctors, nurses, therapists, and medical science. Bud invented and built therapeutic equipment to make breathing easier, and, because of this, Bill Ray seemed to manage better than most.

Before he died, he was able to graduate from technical college with a degree in electronics, although his schooling was punctuated by incessant hospital stays. He had an avid interest in astronomy, building his own telescope from scratch and constructing a computer at a time when computers were still in the developmental stages. When Bud was called to be a bishop, the first person he told was Bill Ray by sending him a message on his homemade computer. Bill Ray showed great courage and faith as, one by one, his friends with cystic fibrosis died in their teens and early twenties. He was an inspiration to others throughout his twenty-eight years here on the earth.

In the more than thirty-five years since the birth of their first child, Margaret and Bud have learned a great deal about happiness, about faith, and, most of all, about hope.

As a young married couple they experienced much sorrow, grief, and heartbreak. Although they wept many tears, they were surprised to find that they were still happy. Even death, the event many fear most, only intensified the joy they received from knowing that they would be together again as an eternal family.

When they were first married, they cherished their nice clothes, popularity, and good times. They went into marriage somewhat spoiled and frivolous. All of that changed with the birth of their children. They suddenly matured and came to realize that life has a much deeper meaning than careers or material possessions. They found that hope became their most important possession and that there was no other place to turn for that hope than the gospel of Jesus Christ.

They found that they were never alone—always the Spirit guided, comforted, and supported them from day to day—through the long hours spent in hospitals, in doctors' waiting rooms, through the good news and the bad. They came to marvel at the peace that "passeth understanding."

Margaret and Bud found that miracles really do happen. No, there were no miraculous healings, no little limbs made whole, no disease-ravished bodies restored to health. But miraculous support came in many ways. Soon hospital and medical care ballooned far out of their income range, but every time one financial door closed, another door opened. Even insurance companies bent their rules and helped financially though they were not obligated to.

Above all, Margaret and Bud received spiritual support. They learned to live one day at a time, guided by the companionship of the Holy Ghost. It became a natural part of their home life, when confronted by a problem or a question, to "go ask the Lord." The answer always came.

Their two remaining children, Margaret and Robin, are now adults and still have a close companionship with the Spirit. Bud and Margaret and their children have been given the assurance that those children from whom they have been parted by death are just as much a part of their family as if they had lived. The four of them look forward to the Resurrection when they will be able to reunite as a family again.

Teaching Ideas and Related Scriptures

Courage: This is a good story to emphasize that many people are not healed from physical ailments, yet they receive help and love from Heavenly Father in many other ways. As Margaret and her husband and children had courage to face their problems, the Lord gave them strength.

Psalm 31:24. "Be of good courage, and he shall strengthen your heart, all ye that hope in the Lord." (*See also* 1 Chronicles 28:20; Psalm 27:14.)

Happiness: The fact that Margaret and Bud were happy in spite of their problems could be used to open a discussion of the difference between momentary pleasure, real happiness, and the sources of each.

Proverbs 16:20. "He that handleth a matter wisely shall find good: and whoso trusteth in the Lord, happy is he." (*See also* James 5:11; Mosiah 2:41.)

Hope and Opposition: This story can be used to demonstrate how adversity and opposition can help us grow, and how hope instead of despair can come from problems.

2 Nephi 31:20. "Wherefore, ye must press forward with a steadfastness in Christ, having a perfect brightness of hope, and a love of God and of all men. Wherefore, if ye shall press forward, feasting upon the word of Christ, and endure to the end, behold, thus saith the Father: Ye shall have eternal life." (*See also* 2 Nephi 2:11; Ether 12:4; D&C 58:4; D&C 122:7.)

Find Her

Be thou humble; and the
Lord thy God shall lead thee
by the hand, and give thee
answer to thy prayers.

D&C 112:10

One night, Bette had a dream about a little girl and was told to find her. She realized that this was not going to be easy, because she only saw the girl from the back. Bette recorded in her journal that she seemed to be about six or seven years old and had long, dark, wavy hair down to her waist. She also seemed to have something wrong with her leg, because she was standing like it was hurt or handicapped.

Bette lived with her husband and family in Florida at the time. They already had four little children—ages six months, two, four, and five years old. They finally decided to approach an adoption agency because they didn't know any other way to find the little girl. After several months, they were accepted as worthy candidates to adopt a child. But they couldn't find her.

They waited for two years in Florida searching through hundreds of little faces in books of children awaiting adoption. They didn't feel that she was among any of them. They were then asked to transfer to San Diego, California. They prayed about it and didn't feel that it was the place in which they belonged. When they also turned down Mesa, Arizona, and asked for a transfer to Utah, they were told that there was only a one percent chance they would be able to move there.

They continued to pray for a move to Utah. When Bette's husband received a call at work and was told they could transfer to Tooele, Utah, he accepted immediately. He just felt it was right for his family.

They quickly called the adoption agency, thinking that the adoption records could be transferred. They were told that they would have to start the process all over again when they got to Utah. Bette was afraid that some day she would have to face Heavenly Father and tell him that she hadn't found the child he told her about. But she didn't really feel that he was giving her a lot of help. Later she came to realize just how wrong she was.

Shortly after arriving in Utah, Bette discovered that she was expecting; they decided that this would be the little girl that she had seen. September found them with a new son instead.

Then her life was filled with complications. A teenage nephew moved in with them, thus raising her family to six children. She was called to be the ward Young Women's president, and a few weeks later developed a painful arthritic condition. She thought to herself that Heavenly Father would understand if she didn't pursue finding the little girl for a little while. By then things would surely settle down a little.

A few weeks later, her Young Women's counselor called to say that a badly abused girl had been brought into the medical center she worked in. She had been beaten with a two-by-four until most of her body was a seeping purple bruise. The counselor felt that she and her husband should become foster parents to the little girl. She was going to call her husband that night who was out of town with his work.

The counselor called the following day a little confused and said that her husband had told her that with their other obligations they wouldn't be able to spend the necessary time with a child that would need so much help. She couldn't understand why she had felt so strongly about being a foster parent to the abused girl. Both Bette and her counselor thought it was a little strange. Two days after her counselor had called, the still, small voice quit whispering and started shouting at Bette. The message was, "That is the little girl you've been looking for!"

Bette called her friend for a description of the girl and was told that she had dark hair down to her waist and was about six or seven years old. Her friend said that she could not tell Bette more, because she had only seen the girl from the back.

The next day Bette called the local family services, who told her that the girl was in temporary custody and would be returned to her natural family within the month. Bette felt confused but somewhat relieved because of her other pressures.

Just one week later, family services called Bette back. They said that the girl's situation had changed and they needed someone to take her in a long-term placement situation. Because Bette worked part-time in the office next door to theirs and they had come to know her, they said they could skip the necessary paper work and waiting period.

Leslie was placed in their home two days later. Family services told them that this was definitely a temporary placement. They also stressed that adoption was very unlikely.

Two and one-half years later, Leslie was adopted by Bette and her husband. Two weeks after that she was sealed to her new family in the Salt Lake Temple. One of the most spiritually stirring moments that those parents have ever experienced happened that day following the sealing. Leslie, dressed in a beautiful white dress, went around the sealing room hugging each person that was there and expressing to each one of them how much she loved them.

Bette learned a great lesson from this experience. She thought Heavenly Father wasn't helping to find Leslie, but he had to get the family transferred to Tooele and have Bette called as the ward Young Women's president so she could call as her counselor the person who worked at the medical clinic. He then had to help Bette become friends with the family services people so they would accept her as a foster mother on the spot. Now when Bette wonders if her prayers are being answered, she remembers this experience and waits patiently for the answer to come.

Teaching Ideas and Related Scriptures

Prayer and Patience: Many of us want immediate answers to our prayers. This story can be used to help teach us to be more patient and have more confidence in the Lord. It demonstrates how the Lord is constantly trying to put us in a position where we can best help ourselves and others. Just because we cannot see what is happening behind the scenes does not mean God is not answering our prayers.

D&C 112:10. "Be thou humble; and the Lord thy God shall lead thee by the hand, and give thee answer to thy prayers." *(See also* Hebrews 6:12; D&C 98:2.)

God's Foreknowledge: This story is a good illustration of how God has the whole picture before him. We as mortals only have pieces of the puzzle and must put them together one at a time.

1 Nephi 9:6. "But the Lord knoweth all things from the beginning; wherefore, he prepareth a way to accomplish all his works among the children of men; for behold, he hath all power unto the fulfilling of all his words." *(See also* 2 Nephi 2:24; D&C 38:2.)

God Knows and Loves Each of Us: Sometimes it is difficult to appreciate how much God is involved in our lives. By focusing the story on Leslie, we can teach how much God loves each of us individually. Look how many things he did so that Leslie would have a good home and the blessings of eternity. He knows and loves each of us as individuals also and is working on our behalf.

1 Nephi 22:25. "And he gathereth his children from the four quarters of the earth; and he numbereth his sheep, and they know him; and there shall be one fold and one shepherd; and he shall feed his sheep, and in him they shall find pasture." *(See also* 2 Nephi 1:15; Alma 26:37.)

Stop!

Be thou humble; and the Lord thy God shall lead thee by the hand, and give thee answer to thy prayers.

D&C 112:10

Some days we wonder if we would have been better off by staying in bed. Max, an employee for a river expedition company, experienced one of those days. It was his job to help take people and equipment to the point of departure for the river trips and to pick them up when they had finished their trip. On this particular day he was to leave Moab, Utah, go up the Colorado River to put a one-day trip in, and then proceed up the river to Cisco, Utah, to pick up another group of people that was finishing. The manager of the local operation, Wayne, was to accompany him that day.

The boat, along with the other gear needed for the one-day trip, was loaded. They noticed that it was especially hot that July day as they arrived at the location for the trip to begin. As Wayne and Max inflated the boat for the trip, the troubles of the day began. Because of the especially hot day, the boat exploded, leaving a three-foot rip in its side. It was decided that Max would have to return to the warehouse and get another boat. By the time the one-day trip was on its way, Wayne and Max were two hours late leaving to pick up the people that were arriving at Cisco. Wayne went ahead in the van that was to haul the people. Max followed in the "boat truck." When Max pulled into the take-out spot, he knew there was more trouble. It was three o'clock in the afternoon, and the group should have been there by one o'clock, but there was no one there. All he saw as he drove up was Wayne standing holding an oar and talking to two kayakers. Wayne then told Max the bad news. The kayakers had given him the oar. They said it was at Skull Rapid that they had last seen the two boats they were to pick up. The first boat through the rapid had tipped over. The kayakers had picked up the oar as it floated down the river. They thought that everyone was all right. The other boat was still above the rapid when they left. So it now was only a matter of waiting. By five o'clock the first boat arrived at the take-out. The people were soaked but safe. The only problem was that the other boat was not with them. They said that the last time that they had seen the other boat was when they went through the rapid. They did not see the second boat go through the rapid.

Max went up a little hill to watch for the second boat to come in. Two hours went by and there was no sign of the boat. About seven o'clock Max spotted a man walking towards him from a distance. He noticed that it was Bill, one of the boatmen from the second boat. He could see that Bill was carrying a water cooler with him. Max quickly ran toward Bill to find out what had happened. Bill explained that as they had attempted to go through Skull Rapid they had gotten caught in a big back-eddy. The swirling water just kept the boat going around and around. The current from the eddy was so strong that they could not get out. All they could do was to maneuver the boat close to the shore and jump out of the boat one at a time. After everybody was out of the boat they then decided to walk down the river to the take-out. The only problem was that after walking for about a mile they came to an area where the river ran against a sheer cliff. There was no way to get around. Bill had decided to empty the water cooler and use it as a float device and float past the cliff so he could get help for the rest of the people. He floated in the river for a couple of miles until he came to a spot where he could again walk on the shore.

At this point, Max and Bill decided that maybe they could get to the people by hiking up over the terrain with some life jackets. When they got to the others they could put the jackets on and float through the river also. They got in the truck and drove up the river for a couple of miles until the road ended. Then they started to hike. This ended up being more difficult than they had expected. Time after time as they hiked, they came to dead ends because of sheer cliffs. Some were as much as thousand-foot drop-offs. After hiking for two and a half hours, they came to a spot where they could see the people. The only problem was that they looked like ants. Max and Bill were a thousand feet above them with no way to get down. They decided that they had better get back to the truck because it was getting dark quickly. They turned and started walking back the way they had come. After walking for a few minutes, it got so dark that neither of them could see more than a couple of feet in front of them, but they continued to walk. Then all of a sudden, Max heard a voice speak to his mind, saying, "Stop!" He turned to Bill to say that they needed to stop, but before he could say anything Bill spoke up, "We need to stop." They decided that they would stop there and spend the night. When it became daylight they would then hike out and get help. They both tried to get some sleep, but it was hard to sleep, especially since they had no water and both of them were very thirsty.

About two-thirty the moon came up. They could now see, so they decided to get up and hike out. As they started to walk the direction they had been walking hours before, they walked only a few feet to find a sheer drop off. If they had not stopped, they would have walked right off the cliff. As they looked at the cliff they both expressed gratitude to Heavenly Father for his guiding hand. They then changed direction and started out the best they knew how. They were not sure which way the truck was, but Max offered a prayer in his heart that Heavenly Father would lead them to the truck. As they hiked they just seemed to know when to turn and what direction to go. It took them thirty minutes to get to the truck. It had taken them two and a half hours in the light to get from the truck to the cliff. Truly the Lord had performed two miracles that night.

Max was very grateful for the happy ending to his otherwise disastrous day. The next day, the rest of the people were rescued safely.

Teaching Ideas and Related Scriptures

Divine Guidance: This story is a good example of how the Lord can lead us from danger and on to safety. Sometimes we need to just let him guide us, not knowing beforehand where to go or what to do.

1 Nephi 4:6. "And I was led by the Spirit, not knowing beforehand the things which I should do." (*See also* Proverbs 3:5–6; D&C 78:18; D&C 112:10.)

You Can Have Anything You Ask For

Pray always, and I will pour out my Spirit upon you, and great shall be your blessing—yea, even more than if you should obtain treasures of earth and corruptibleness to the extent thereof.

D&C 19:38

Beth, a senior student in seminary, approached her teacher one morning and asked if she could bear her testimony to the class. Her teacher was more than happy to let her, so after the devotional Beth got up and told the following story to the class.

When Beth was ten years old, she was the only active Church member in her family. One day in Primary her teacher gave a lesson on the power of prayer and told the students that Heavenly Father would answer and grant any prayer if it was right for them and done in faith.

Ten-year-old Beth was so inspired by this lesson that when she got home she immediately went to her room, knelt down by her bed, and began to pray. She said, "Heavenly Father, you know my father is a good man and a good father, but he never goes to church—not even when I have a part on the program. Oh, Heavenly Father, please touch my father's heart so he will have the desire to go to church so we can become an eternal family."

Several times every day Beth would kneel down and plead with the Lord that he would touch her father so he would become active in the church and go through the temple. Beth pleaded with the Lord every day for six years. Sometimes she would break down and cry as she pleaded with her Heavenly Father in behalf of her earthly father.

Three or four days before Beth's sixteenth birthday, the family was sitting around the breakfast table. Beth's father asked her what she would like for her birthday. He was a fairly well-to-do building contractor and had purchased Beth's sister a new car for her sixteenth birthday just a year before. He told her that she could have anything she wanted and that money was no problem.

Beth was about ready to discuss the prospect of a new car when a voice came into her mind and said, "Beth, here is your chance! Here is what you have been hoping for and praying for all of these years!" Beth paused for a few seconds and said, "Dad, there is one thing I would like to have more than anything else in this world, and it won't cost you one penny."

Her father almost fell off of his chair and wanted to know what this marvelous thing was that would not cost him anything. Beth said that she would not tell him until he had promised her that he would give it to her. Her father didn't feel that that was fair, but she would not tell him what she wanted. Then her mother and older sister tried to get her to tell what she wanted, but she said that she would not until her Dad promised to give it to her. Even her two little brothers said that she was being unfair, but she refused to say what she wanted until her Dad promised.

Seeing that Beth was not going to give in, her father finally said, "All right, I promise!" Beth said, "Dad, the one thing I want more than anything else in this world is that we kneel down every morning together as a family in family prayer." Her father later said that it was like someone dropped a ton of bricks on him—he just sat there stunned. It was a request he had least expected but knew he must fulfill in order to maintain his integrity with Beth.

The next morning, true to his word, the father called the family together for family prayer. He called upon Beth to give the prayer because she was the only one in the family that was active. Beth gave the prayer every morning for the first week. After about a week, the mother said that she would be willing to take a turn and lead the family in prayer. Beth's older sister was the next family member to decide that she could take her turn praying. Then her two little brothers began to pray.

After about a month, as the family knelt for prayer one morning, there was a pause for a moment and then the father said, "I guess it's about my turn to pray.'' Beth said as her father began to pray, tears welled up in her eyes and rolled down her cheeks. She felt that she was hearing the most humble and beautiful prayer that had ever been expressed by the lips of a mortal man. It was wonderful! It was the first time she had ever heard her father pray, and the spiritual effect it had upon the whole family was overwhelming. When the prayer was over, the whole family came together in one big hug of emotion and wept in gratitude for the great blessing that had come into their home.

Beth then told the class that yesterday had been her seventeenth birthday. She said that she had received the most beautiful gift that any mortal could ever receive. Her family had gotten up early and driven fifty miles to the Salt Lake Temple. She had then been ushered into the most beautiful room she had ever been in and had knelt at a holy altar there with her family. As Beth, her brothers and sister, and parents had held hands across a holy altar, they took an important step towards becoming an eternal family. By this time, all of the students, along with Beth and the teacher, were in tears as they shared together the sweet spirit of the Lord.

Beth was so grateful for a Primary teacher who had taught her the importance of prayer. She had learned that some prayers may be answered the same day but that some prayers may take six years or more before they are answered. She had also learned the important roles that faith and persistence play in successful prayers. She was so grateful that she had not asked for a car or for some other material gift but had received the help and the prompting of the Holy Ghost that important morning around the breakfast table.

Teaching Ideas and Related Scriptures

Church Service: Sometimes we don't realize the value and importance of our service in the Church. The Primary teacher in this story probably has no idea of the influence her one lesson has had on Beth and her family as the children of that class have grown, gone on missions, served in the Church, and had children of their own. Literally hundreds, if not thousands, of people will be effected because of this one faithful Primary teacher.

D&C 18:10, 15-16. "Remember the worth of souls is great in the sight of God. . . .

"And if it so be that you should labor all your days in crying repentance unto this people, and bring, save it be one soul unto me, how great shall be your joy with him in the kingdom of my Father!

"And now, if your joy will be great with one soul that you have brought unto me into the kingdom of my Father, how great will be your joy if you should bring many souls unto me!"

Family; Children Helping Parents: Parents have the responsibility of teaching the gospel to their children, but sometimes the opposite happens. This story could be shared to encourage those with inactive parents to help them instead of just giving up on them.

Alma 32:23. "And now, he imparteth his word by angels unto men, yea, not only men but women also. Now this is not all; little children do have words given unto them many times, which confound the wise and the learned." (*See also* Malachi 4:6; Matthew 18:3-4; Mosiah 3:19.)

Eternal Family: Someone had planted into Beth's heart the importance of an eternal family. Many times we overlook the promptings of the Spirit that fill the hearts of children with the desire to be sealed to their parents.

D&C 138:47-48. "The Prophet Elijah was to plant in the hearts of the children the promises made to their fathers,

"Foreshadowing the great work to be done in the temples of the Lord in the dispensation of the fulness of times, for the redemption of the dead, and the sealing of the children to their parents, lest the whole earth be smitten with a curse and utterly wasted at his coming. (*See also D&C* 130:2; *D&C* 131:2-4.)

Prayer and Patience: This story illustrates that when Heavenly Father is working with the agency of people, it may take years to receive an answer to a prayer. We need to be careful that we do not promise that every person we pray for will respond. Heavenly Father will not take away a person's agency. On the other hand, our own righteous prayers can have a great effect on those we love. We can also receive the help that we need to say the right thing at the right time.

3 Nephi 18:20. "And whatsoever ye shall ask the Father in my name, which is right, believing that ye shall receive, behold it shall be given unto you." (*See also* Alma 34:27; D&C 19:38; D&C 98:2; D&C 112:10.)

Family Prayer: As we read this story of a sixteen-year-old girl who would rather have family prayer than a new car or any other worldly possession, it helps put the importance of family prayer in perspective.

3 Nephi 18:21. "Pray in your families unto the Father, always in my name, that your wives and your children may be blessed." (*See also* Alma 34:27; D&C 29:6.)

Priorities: Every day of our lives we have to choose between the things of God and the things of this world. Beth's choice of family prayer instead of a car is an excellent example of choosing the kingdom of God over the things of the world.

D&C 19:38. "Pray always, and I will pour out my Spirit upon you, and great shall be your blessing—yea, even more than if you should obtain treasures of earth and corruptibleness to the extent thereof." (*See also* Matthew 6:19–20; Matthew 6:33; Matthew 13:44–46.)

Send Kenny

Children, obey your
parents in all things: for this
is well pleasing unto the Lord.

Colossians 3:20

It was a chilly October morning. The Molgard children were out
of school for the annual Utah deer hunt, but their family had
chosen to spend the time at a family cabin in Alpine, Wyoming.
Dad, Grandpa, Uncle Jack, and brother Max had gone fishing
on the Palisades Reservoir. The mother, Bette, was trying to
finish reading the Book of Mormon while five children were
cooped up in the cabin due to heavy rainfall and cold mountain
temperatures. After several hours of storminess, the skies
cleared and Bette suggested the children put on their coats and
go down to the lake to see if the men had caught any fish. Two
girls wanted to go and so did four-year-old McKay. Ten-year-
old Kenny said he'd rather just hang around the cabin.

Bette clearly heard a still, small voice say, "Kenny has to
go." When she asked Kenny if he would, he strongly objected.
He just didn't want to go. The other children started to go, and
the voice came again, "Kenny needs to go." Another plea, and
the same response. Seeing that tougher tactics were needed,
Bette demanded that Kenny go. He stomped out of the cabin,
and Bette thought the case was settled. But when the children
got to the road, Kenny wasn't with them. Bette found him hiding beside the cabin and threatened to withhold lunch if he
didn't do as he was told. Kenny angrily huffed after the others.

He was soon into the spirit of the walk. He and McKay
picked up rocks and stuffed the best ones in their pockets.
When they arrived at the lake, the boat was on the other side,
out of sight. The children decided to play by the water and wait

73

until it came back. Kenny continued gathering and throwing rocks, and McKay went to play on a wooden dock that was connected to the shore and floated out onto the water for about twenty feet. When he got to the end of the dock, he began to toss rocks into the water. As he bent over to observe a school of small fish, the waves of a nearby motor boat rocked the dock. McKay lost his balance and fell into the murky, ice-cold water. Kenny saw McKay go in and, without hesitating, went into the lake and swam the twenty feet to his little brother. By the time he got to him, McKay was about a foot under the water. Kenny dived under him and pushed McKay's head up out of the water. Leaving his own head below, Kenny kicked as hard as he could until his sisters were able to grab McKay at the dock.

Kenny's method of rescue saved not only his brother's life, but perhaps his own. Because of the small weight differential (about twenty-five pounds) and Kenny's limited lifesaving skills, there was a strong possibility that the two brothers could have latched onto each other and neither one made it back to shore or the dock.

Kenny learned a great lesson about obeying his parents and received the Boy Scout Medal of Merit for saving his brother's life. Bette gratefully promised herself that she would always listen and act on the whisperings of the still, small voice.

Teaching Ideas and Related Scriptures

Honoring Father and Mother: As children obey their parents, the Lord will bless them. If Kenny had not eventually obeyed his mother, his brother probably would have drowned.

Exodus 20:12. "Honour thy father and thy mother: that thy days may be long upon the land which the Lord thy God giveth thee." (*See also* Colossians 3:20.)

Revelation and the Holy Ghost: Revelation by the power of the Holy Ghost is a very real thing that all God's children can receive to guide their personal lives.

2 Nephi 32:5. "For behold, again I say unto you that if ye will enter in by the way, and receive the Holy Ghost, it will show unto you all things what ye should do."

"Please Don't Talk About My Fireplace"

And I give unto you a commandment that you shall teach one another the doctrine of the kingdom.

D&C 88:77

Richard, the elders quorum instructor in his ward, was sitting in a presidency meeting when he heard of Pete's refusal to have home teachers visit his family. As the quorum presidency discussed this problem, Richard found himself volunteering to be Pete's home teacher. He was told that Pete was not a Latter-day Saint but that his wife and children were active members and really wanted Pete to join the Church. In fact, because of his wife's great desire for Pete to join, she may have been pushing too hard and seemed to be driving him further away from the Church.

As Richard pondered his new assignment, he felt that he should first sit down with Pete and find out what he desired for his family. He wanted Pete to know that he respected his role of husband and father whether or not he was a member of the Church.

A few days later, Pete showed up at the bank where Richard worked, so he invited Pete into the conference room for a private discussion. Because Pete was a nonmember, Richard asked him if he knew what home teachers were. Pete said that he had had them for years. When Richard said that he was Pete's new home teacher, Pete asked him not to come into his home. He said that he was tired of talking about his new fireplace. When Richard asked what his fireplace had to do with home teaching, Pete explained that his home teachers would come each month and sit on the couch. They would look nervously around for a few minutes and then tell him what a good job he had done on his fireplace. They would talk about his fireplace for a while and then leave. Next month they would repeat the process—this had been going on for over six months. Pete indicated that he was really quite bored with hearing about his fireplace.

Richard promised that he would not come to Pete's house until he was invited, and, since he hadn't even seen his fireplace, he would not talk about it. He told Pete that he would like to contact him in other ways and would not contact his wife or children. Pete felt okay about this and they parted. For the next several months Richard met with Pete in his pick-up truck and at the bank. He took him to lunch and played tennis with him several times. He just got to know him well: Pete and Richard became very close friends.

Pete had three daughters and one son. His oldest daughter, Vicky, was seven. Richard suggested to Pete one day that it would be appropriate for his daughter to be baptized when she turned eight and asked him how he felt about her being baptized. Pete told him that he would really like that. Richard then surprised him by suggesting that Pete do the baptizing. When Pete replied that he couldn't do it because he was not a member, Richard suggested that his nonmember status could be quickly taken care of. Pete declined, saying that he wasn't ready yet, and asked Richard to baptize his daughter. There was a very good spirit at the baptismal service, and Pete enjoyed it a great deal.

During this period of time Richard became the elders quorum president. He continued to home teach Pete but still had never been to Pete's house. In fact, one of Pete's neighbors contacted Richard, because he was the quorum president, and gave him a message from Pete's wife reporting that they did not have any home teachers.

When Pete's grandfather passed away, he wanted to come over and talk to Richard about it. They went into Richard's backyard and spent a couple of hours talking about where his grandfather was and what had happened to him. Richard had the opportunity to share with Pete the beautiful plan of salvation. This seemed to be the time when Pete really began to soften his heart and desire to accept the gospel.

Pete and Richard continued to meet often as close friends while Pete was taught the gospel. Late one Thursday night, nine months after Richard had become Pete's home teacher, Pete called and asked Richard to baptize him. Needless to say, Richard was very excited and asked if Saturday would be okay. Pete agreed, so Richard called the bishop and other priesthood leaders to get the baptism arranged and the "word out" among ward members. That Saturday, 110 members showed up to see Pete baptized. Pete was the main speaker at his own baptism and told the story of his conversion. It was a very touching experience for Pete and those present as he bore his testimony of the gospel and thanked Richard and others for what they had done.

One year later Richard and his wife sat in a sealing room of the temple and watched Pete's family kneel around the altar and be sealed as an eternal family. Now Pete is a home teacher himself and accepts home teachers into his home as well as accepting other positions of service in the Church.

To this day Richard still feels that the key to Pete's conversion was respecting his responsibility as a husband and father and just becoming a close friend. Even though Pete and Richard now live in different communities, they and their wives are still close and keep in contact with each other.

Teaching Ideas and Related Scriptures

Home Teaching: The Church has always stressed the importance of working through the father with any contact we have with a family. This especially holds true when it comes to home teaching. When we ignore the father and teach his family without him or embarrass him in front of his family by discussing gospel principles he doesn't live, it really slows down our effectiveness in helping him become active. This story also illustrates the importance of bringing a gospel message and not just wasting the family's time. In order to teach the gospel, and include the father, home teachers need to always sit down with the father first and find out what he would like them to do for him and for his family. Working with the father always pays off in the long run.

D&C 38:23-24. "But, verily I say unto you, teach one another according to the office wherewith I have appointed you;

"And let every man esteem his brother as himself, and practice virtue and holiness before me." (*See also* D&C 20:46-47; D&C 88:77.)

Go to the Third Floor

And it came to pass that the Lord commanded them that they should go forth into the wilderness, yea, into that quarter where there never had man been. And it came to pass that the Lord did go before them, and did talk with them as he stood in a cloud, and gave directions whither they should travel.

Ether 2:5

As the morning began, Elder Kelly and Elder George knelt together as companions and asked Heavenly Father to lead them to those who had been prepared to hear the gospel. After spending two or three unsuccessful hours knocking on doors, they returned to their car knowing they must go somewhere else. After deciding to offer another prayer, they again pleaded with Heavenly Father to help them to know where to go. When they had concluded their prayer they sat in their car, wondering where to go next. As they both looked at a large apartment building some two miles away by the ocean side, they turned to each other and said, "That is where we are to go." They quickly drove to the apartment building and parked their car. It was an attractive, three-story building. The two missionaries entered the apartment complex and began to systematically knock on each apartment door. After knocking on every door on the first floor, they had not found even one person home. They went to the second floor and suffered the same results. Both missionaries now doubted that this was where they were to be. In fact, they turned to each other and said, "Let's go."

As they started down the stairs, however, the Spirit spoke clearly to Elder George's mind: "Go up to the third floor." Elder George was walking behind Elder Kelly and they reached the parking lot before Elder George could get up enough courage to say, "We need to go back to the third floor." To his surprise, Elder Kelly immediately agreed. They climbed the stairs once again, this time going to the third floor. Again, as on the other floors, no one was home. They knocked on every door with no success, until there was just one door left. When they knocked on this door, to their surprise, the door actually opened and a man greeted them. As Elder George introduced Elder Kelly and himself as missionaries representing The Church of Jesus Christ of Latter-day Saints, the man said, "I know, I saw you come to my door in a dream. Come in and tell me more."

Teaching Ideas and Related Scriptures

Dreams: One means by which the Lord speaks to men is through dreams.

Acts 2:17. "And it shall come to pass in the last days, saith God, I will pour out of my Spirit upon all flesh: and your sons and your daughters shall prophesy, and your young men shall see visions, and your old men shall dream dreams." (*See also* Joel 2:28.)

Divine Guidance; Lead, Guide and Direct: If we are prayerful, the Lord will give us the guidance that we need.

Proverbs 3:5-6. "Trust in the Lord with all thine heart; and lean not unto thine own understanding.

"In all thy ways acknowledge him, and he shall direct thy paths." (*See also* Isaiah 48:17; Ether 2:5; Moroni 6:9.)

Left Behind

And there shall be silence in heaven for the space of half an hour; and immediately after shall the curtain of heaven be unfolded, as a scroll is unfolded after it is rolled up, and the face of the Lord shall be unveiled;

And the saints that are upon the earth, who are alive, shall be quickened and be caught up to meet him.

D&C 88:95–96

Craig had always wondered what the second coming of Christ would be like. He had spent many hours thinking and reading about it. Then, one night when he was seventeen years old, he had an experience that helped him realize what it may be like to be here when the Savior comes.

Craig had a dream that was so real that twenty years later he still remembers it clearly. In his dream he found himself in a dark but large park or open space. The park was full of people milling around, but he didn't recognize anyone. There was a feeling of excitement and great expectation. The people's anticipation was so great that the air felt like it was charged with electricity.

Suddenly, amid the rumbling of thunder and great bolts of lightning, the black sky parted and Jesus appeared in a brilliant light. Even though the Savior was very far away, Craig saw his features as though he was standing next to him. He realized that Christ didn't look like any picture that he had ever seen.

Even though Craig's eyes never left the Savior's face, he was aware that everyone else was staring intently at the Savior also. Soon some of the people around Craig were lifted up off the ground. He noticed one here and one there until more and more of them were lifted up to meet the Savior.

Craig suddenly became aware of the fact that he had not moved at all. An extremely empty, brokenhearted feeling then came over him as he realized that he was being left behind and was not worthy to meet the Savior. He can still remember those feelings of total emptiness and rejection.

Craig started to pray and plead that the Savior would lift him up and not leave him behind. He had such a strong desire to be lifted up that he even began jumping to try to get off the ground and begin the process of being lifted up.

Craig finally gave up and just stood there in total despair. Suddenly he felt himself leave the ground, and an overwhelming sense of relief, happiness, and satisfaction filled his soul. He even breathed an audible sigh of relief and shouted to himself, "I made it! I made it!"

Of the many dreams that Craig has had, this is the only one that he remembers in detail and with great emotion. He feels that this dream was given to him to teach him the importance of preparing for the Second Coming. Now that he has experienced the feelings of both being left behind and being lifted up, he is working hard to be worthy to meet the Savior when he comes.

Teaching Ideas and Related Scriptures

Revelation and Dreams: You could use this story to illustrate that dreams are still being received today. Support this concept with stories from the scriptures that deal with dreams.

Matthew 1:20–21. "But while he thought on these things, behold, the angel of the Lord appeared unto him in a dream, saying, Joseph, thou son of David, fear not to take unto thee Mary thy wife: for that which is conceived in her is of the Holy Ghost.

"And she shall bring forth a son, and thou shalt call his name JESUS: for he shall save his people from their sins." (*See also* Genesis 37 [Joseph as a boy]; Genesis 40 [Joseph in prison]; Genesis 41 [Joseph and Pharaoh]; 1 Kings 3:5–14 [Solomon]; Matthew 2 [wise men and Joseph]; 1 Nephi 2:2 [Lehi].)

Second Coming: This story could be used in several ways in teaching about the Second Coming:

(1) To illustrate how the righteous will be caught up to meet the Savior when he comes.

(2) To illustrate how it would feel to be ready to meet the Savior, and how it would feel to be left behind when others close to us are being lifted up.

(3) As a lesson starter to get the students interested into turning to the scriptures to see whether the dream was accurate.

(4) As a lesson conclusion to help the students better feel what it might be like to be here for the Second Coming and to help them desire to better prepare for this great event.

D&C 38:8. "But the day soon cometh that ye shall see me, and know that I am; for the veil of darkness shall soon be rent, and he that is not purified shall not abide the day." (*See also* D&C 29:11; D&C 39:20–22; D&C 45:56–58; D&C 76:102–105; D&C 88:95–96.)

Not Now

But with some I am not well pleased, for they will not open their mouths, but they hide the talent which I have given unto them, because of the fear of man. Wo unto such, for mine anger is kindled against them.

D&C 60:2

Elders Carnes and Morgan had taught a late discussion. They were hurrying home because they were already late in getting back to their apartment. As they drove along the streets of Los Angeles they passed a liquor store. They saw that the store was closed and noticed a man messing with the front door. As they drove by, he looked at them and they at him. They then heard the burglar alarm on the store go off. As soon as they were around the corner and out of sight of the man, they stopped the car. Elder Morgan turned to Elder Carnes and said that he thought the man was trying to break into the liquor store. Elder Carnes agreed and suggested that they turn around and see what the man was really up to. They turned the car around and cautiously pulled up in front of the store on the opposite side of the street. They saw that the man was now inside the store and that the burglar alarm had been turned off. They could see the man hiding down behind the counter. He kept peeking over the counter and looking very nervously at them.

After some discussion Elder Carnes and Elder Morgan decided they would wait for a police car to come by and try to stop it. After about two minutes of waiting, which seemed like an eternity to the two excited Elders, the man reached up from behind the counter and grabbed the phone. This really made the missionaries uneasy, and they were afraid that he was calling someone to come by and "take care of them."

After about five minutes of waiting, someone did just that. A police car with two policemen came down the street. Elder Carnes waved his arm out of the window to signal the policemen to stop. The police car backed up and quickly pulled in behind the Elders' car. To the surprise of both Elder Carnes and Elder Morgan, as they got out of their car and tried to explain about the man in the liquor store, the policemen yelled for them to get up against the car. Each policeman took a missionary and began to search him.

The policemen told them that the man inside the store was the owner and that he had been robbed two nights before. He had called the police, because he thought the missionaries were the robbers returning to kill him. Then more police cars arrived, and it was apparent to the missionaries that they were in serious trouble. They couldn't even find the registration to the mission car. All they had was their missionary identification and their driver's licenses.

As the policemen interrogated the missionaries separately, Elder Morgan received an unusual request from the Spirit. As soon as the officer came up to him, the Spirit prompted, "Ask him about the Church." Elder Morgan's response was, "Not now, this is not a good time to ask about the Church!" As the policeman asked him questions, the Spirit spoke again with the same message. Again Elder Morgan responded that this was poor timing and definitely the wrong time to ask a policeman about the Church. When the officers had gathered all the information they needed, the one who had questioned Elder Carnes went to the car and radioed the dispatcher to check on the car registration and verify the story that had been given by the missionaries. As he was doing this, the officer with Elder Morgan asked him what he did as a missionary. Elder Morgan told him that they visited with people and taught them about the Church. For the third time, the Spirit spoke and said, "Ask him about the Church!" This time Elder Morgan responded and asked him if he knew much about the Mormons. He replied that he knew a little and had once dated a girl whose father was a bishop. Elder Morgan then got brave and asked him if he would be interested in having them come by and teach him about the Church. The officer said that he would be very interested. As Elder Morgan opened his appointment book, the officer's partner yelled, "We've got an emergency call, let's go!" and the policeman ran for the car. As the police car sped away, Elder Morgan was left holding the open appointment book with no name and address.

Elder Morgan went home that night in great pain. He pleaded with Heavenly Father and asked him to forgive him for fearing men and circumstance instead of listening to the Holy Ghost. He promised that in the future he would act when the Spirit spoke, regardless of the situation.

Teaching Ideas and Related Scriptures

Fear: Sometimes we fear or respect man more than God. When we do, it only brings disappointment and lost opportunities.

D&C 3:7. "For, behold, you should not have feared man more than God. Although men set at naught the counsels of God, and despise his words—

"Yet you should have been faithful; and he would have extended his arm and supported you against all the fiery darts of the adversary; and he would have been with you in every time of trouble." (*See also* Proverbs 29:25; Isaiah 51:7; 2 Nephi 8:7; D&C 30:11; D&C 60:2.)

Inspiration: The Holy Ghost speaks to our mind and heart in a still, small voice as it did to Elder Morgan. When it does, we must recognize it and then obey its instructions.

Helaman 5:30. "And it came to pass when they heard this voice, and beheld that it was not a voice of thunder, neither was it a voice of a great tumultuous noise, but behold, it was a still small voice of perfect mildness, as if it had been a whisper, and it did pierce even to the very soul." (*See also* D&C 8:2.)

He Helped Someone Every Day

But when thou doest alms let not thy left hand know what thy right hand doeth;

That thine alms may be in secret; and thy Father who seeth in secret, himself shall reward thee openly.

3 Nephi 13:3–4

LaVerne's story is a difficult one to tell because each event in his life was a private matter between LaVerne and those that he helped. He lived in a small Utah community of about 4,000 people. John, a member of this community, still remembers the first time that he became acquainted with LaVerne. John was trying to repair his daughter's bike which needed a new wheel. He was told that it was very likely that LaVerne would have a wheel that would fit. He found LaVerne in his backyard working on one of his current projects. John asked him if he happened to have a wheel that would fit, and LaVerne invited him into his shed to look for one. As John glanced around the shed, he was amazed at the equipment and materials LaVerne had accumulated. The walls were covered with bins, their contents carefully sorted so that things could easily be found.

They found a wheel that fit perfectly, but when John tried to pay for it his money was refused. Before John could leave with the wheel, LaVerne told him to stick around for a minute, grabbed an empty tool box, and began to fill it with tools for John to take home with him. LaVerne would take tools that others had discarded and fix them up. He would put new handles on those that needed them, get rid of the rust that many of them were covered with, and repaint them so they were almost like new. Then he gave most of them away. LaVerne couldn't understand why people threw away so many items that were still usable and needed by others.

As John picked up his tools and headed for his car, LaVerne asked him if he could use another rake and shovel and gave him these tools also. Before John could get into his car, LaVerne told him that if he ever needed anything else to be sure and come back. From that day on, John made many trips to LaVerne's shed, nearly always with success.

A short time later, John was trying to sell his house, but before he could do so he had to have it inspected by termite inspectors. No loans would be given on the house until the banks were sure that it was free from termites. The front part of his house had no basement and the dirt came within eighteen inches of the floor joists. The inspector said that the dirt would have to be dug out from under the house until there was at least a three-foot crawl space so they could get under the house and properly inspect the foundation.

John had no idea how he was going to get the dirt out of there —until one day when he was talking with LaVerne. LaVerne indicated that he would like to come over to his home and look the situation over. The next Saturday morning, he showed up bright and early to see what could be done. They cut a trap door in the kitchen floor. LaVerne then got under the house and, for the next five days, not counting Sunday, became a miniature bulldozer with a little shovel and pick.

The ground was extremely hard and there was little room to use the tools, but LaVerne would lay on his side and dig as hard and as fast as he could. They couldn't even get him to stop and take a break. Once LaVerne started a project, it was full steam ahead until the project was completed. The digging caused so much dust that anyone under the floor had to have handkerchiefs over their nose and mouth in order to breathe. LaVerne would dig the dirt loose and put it into buckets. John's boys would drag the buckets to the kitchen trap door where John would then lift them out of the hole, dump them into a wheelbarrow and scatter the dirt around the backyard. One week later, when the inspector came to the home, he was amazed at the amount of dirt that had been moved by hand. He indicated that most people had to break a hole in the outside wall and rent a conveyor belt in order to get the dirt out from under their homes.

Another person who was blessed by LaVerne's great love to serve was Karma. She had been running a nursery school in an old city building, but the city wanted the building back. That meant that she had to find a new place before the next school year started. She finally bought a home with a basement in it just two weeks before her nursery school was scheduled to begin. Karma and her family had no idea what they were going to do to get the basement remodeled in time—until LaVerne stepped into the picture. He looked the situation over and assured the family that, by working together, they could have the basement ready in time. Thirteen days later, just one day before school started, the job was finished.

Many widows in the community depended upon LaVerne. If they had plumbing or carpentry needs, they turned to him and he was always there. Many of them had no other place to turn and would have suffered serious hardship without his willing assistance. He loved the opportunity to give them the help they needed.

LaVerne also gave much time and service to the Church. He was missionary minded and not only served a full-time mission but also spent many years serving as a stake missionary. No one is sure of how many missionaries LaVerne helped financially, because it was done quietly and secretly, but he was always helping several.

LaVerne served in the ward library for many years. During this period of time, he made over five hundred dioramas that he donated to the Church to aid the teachers in the classrooms. One day, while he was in the library, he overheard the nursery leader mention to somone how difficult it was to carry the boxes of toys to the nursery each week and then carry them back again to the closet on the other side of the chapel. Two weeks later, when the nursery leader entered her classroom, she was amazed to find a wooden toy cabinet on wheels. It opened up into several large shelves and even had a lock on it so it could be kept in the nursery room. When the other ward's nursery leader saw it, she commented on how nice it would be to have one in their ward. It only took LaVerne a week or two to fulfill her needs as well.

A great example of LaVerne's sensitivity and charity centered around a huge playhouse that LaVerne had built for children in his neighborhood. He was told that the property it was on was needed and that it would have to be moved. LaVerne called several families and told them that whoever came and hauled it away first could have it. A family came right down, and their children were so excited when they saw the large beautiful playhouse that would soon be in their yard. The father said that he would borrow a truck and pick the playhouse up the next morning.

When the family came back the next morning, the playhouse was gone. The children were brokenhearted. LaVerne called around and found that another family had picked it up, not realizing that it had been promised to someone else. When LaVerne saw the disappointment in the children's faces, he immediately went to work. A few days later the disappointed family received a phone call and was told to come to LaVerne's and pick up an exact duplicate of the original playhouse. Several other playhouses were later made and dispersed from LaVerne's backyard.

LaVerne was also very generous with his money. He spent very little on himself, and some estimate that he gave between one-half and two-thirds of his income to the Church and to others. Wards and stakes had no boundaries where LaVerne was concerned. When he heard that another ward in the community was having financial problems, within a few days he was on the bishop's doorstep with a thousand dollars to help the ward. LaVerne never had a bank account and always gave financial help in cash, usually in twenty-dollar bills. Only those very close to LaVerne recognized his method of disbursement and marvelled when, time after time, they heard stories of people throughout the community receiving hundreds of dollars in twenty-dollar bills. Invariably this came when these families were in real need.

One reason why LaVerne used cash was that it could not be traced back to him. When his new bishop approached him and told him that his very generous donations to the ward would need to be receipted, LaVerne was upset. He didn't even want the ward clerk or another member of the bishopric to know who was making the donations. After much discussion, he finally accepted the fact that the Church needed proper bookkeeping but pleaded with the bishop to keep his donations completely secret. Many times each year, LaVerne would give large amounts of money to the bishop to dispense to ward members that were in need.

It is not that LaVerne made a great deal of money. The truth is that he never gave a thought to himself. LaVerne's whole existence was for others. His possessions were meager. He never owned a car and cared nothing for the frills we consider necessities. He literally went about doing good, as the Savior did. He did not wait for an opportunity to come to him or for someone to ask for help but searched for a chance to help someone else. LaVerne did more than talk about his concerns, and he used the tools all of us have at our disposal. He used his energy, his time, his talents, and his means.

Because LaVerne was such a private person, we will never know, in this life at least, how much he actually did. We only hear the bits and pieces, echos and reverberations. It is safe to say, however, that LaVerne did something for someone every day of his adult life. It is significant that his last day here on this earth was spent helping someone in need.

Teaching Ideas and Related Scriptures

Almsgiving: The reason why we give is an important part of giving. If we only give for the attention that it brings us, we have received our reward. LaVerne gave out of love, sincere concern, and total unselfishness. Because his motives were pure and good, his giving brought him great joy and satisfaction in this world and blessings in the world to come.

Jacob 2:17. "Think of your brethren like unto yourselves, and be familiar with all and free with your substance, that they may be rich like unto you." (*See also* Matthew 6:1-4; Acts 20:35; Mosiah 4:26; Alma 1:27; 3 Nephi 13:1-4; Moroni 7:6-11.)

Charity and Service: See teaching helps for "Almsgiving" above.

James 1:27. "Pure religion and undefiled before God and the Father is this, To visit the fatherless and widows in their affliction, and to keep himself unspotted from the world." (*See also* Isaiah 1:17; Mosiah 2:17; Mosiah 4:16; Alma 34:28–29; D&C 58:27.)

Generosity: LaVerne died just a few years ago. Discuss LaVerne's unselfish giving. Help those you are teaching see that LaVerne stored up treasure that would not rust while he was here and presumably is now reaping the benefits of his great generosity. If he had spent his time and money on worldly pleasures and possessions, they would be of absolutely no use to him now.

2 Corinthians 9:7. "Every man according as he purposeth in his heart, so let him give; not grudgingly, or of necessity: for God loveth a cheerful giver." (*See also* Proverbs 19:17; Matthew 25:34–45; Mark 12:42–44.)

Priorities: See teaching helps for "Generosity" above.

Matthew 6:19–21. "Lay not up for yourselves treasures upon earth, where moth and rust doth corrupt, and where thieves break through and steal:

"But lay up for yourselves treasures in heaven, where neither moth nor rust doth corrupt, and where thieves do not break through nor steal:

"For where your treasure is, there will your heart be also." (*See also* Luke 12:15–22; James 2:24.)

The Baby Will Be A Girl

And now, he imparteth his word by angels unto men, yea, not only men but women also. Now this is not all; little children do have words given unto them many times, which confound the wise and the learned.

Alma 32:23

While most of the people in the United States were celebrating the Fourth of July, Judy was being rushed to the hospital in an ambulance. After four months of pregnancy with her fourth child, she had suffered a miscarriage and was hemorrhaging badly. Her husband, Steve, called some friends from the hospital and asked them to take care of their three young children; he spent the rest of the day sitting by Judy's bed as she came very close to death. She received one blood transfusion after another until her body finally began to respond, but it was three days before she was strong enough to return home.

Because of this experience, when Judy became pregnant again, Steve and the children were very concerned. They prayed daily that she and the baby would be okay.

One Tuesday evening, Judy was asked to teach the Mia Maid class and left Steve alone with the children. Steve sent Tiffany, their seven-year-old daughter, into her bedroom to say her prayers and get ready for bed. In a few minutes Tiffany came out of her bedroom and said to her father, "Dad, the baby is going to be a girl and everything will be okay."

The dad, very surprised at this statement, asked Tiffany how she knew this. She answered that the Holy Ghost had told her. Tiffany's dad was really curious now and wanted to know how the Holy Ghost had told her. Tiffany explained that while she was praying, a voice had spoken to her and told her about her mother and the baby. The father was still full of questions and asked Tiffany how she knew that it was the Holy Ghost speaking to her. She said that when she first heard the voice it was so clear that it startled her because she thought someone else was in the room with her. When she looked around the room, however, no one was there. She then felt a very peaceful and calm feeling come over her and she felt that, since she couldn't see anyone, it was the Holy Ghost who had spoken to her.

When Judy arrived home later that evening, Steve shared with her the special experience that their daughter had been given. Both of them were grateful to Heavenly Father for the peace and assurance that this brought into their lives and the lives of their children. From that day on, whenever anyone would ask Tiffany what the baby was going to be, she would emphatically say that it would be a girl.

Five months later, when the baby was born, sure enough, it was a girl. Their other three babies had all had jaundice and some had returned to the hospital for treatment, but this baby was their easiest birth and was born with perfect health. When the baby was born and Steve and Judy first saw that it was a girl, they looked at each other and cried again for the sweet blessing that had come into their home that special night when the Holy Ghost had spoken to their seven-year-old daughter.

Teaching Ideas and Related Scriptures

Faith and Purity of Children: This story illustrates the great faith and purity of children and helps to show why adults are commanded to become as children. Because of their great faith, many children seem to experience spiritual contacts with our Father in Heaven.

Alma 32:23. "And now, he imparteth his word by angels unto men, yea, not only men but women also. Now this is not all; little children do have words given unto them many times, which confound the wise and the learned." (*See also* Matthew 18:3-4; Matthew 19:14; Mosiah 3:19.)

Holy Ghost: This story can be used to illustrate that two of the Holy Ghost's functions are to bring comfort and to tell of future events. It also illustrates that, although we usually get feelings or ideas from the Holy Ghost, at times we may actually hear a voice. Whether this voice is vocal or just in our head is sometimes hard to tell.

Jacob 4:13. "For the Spirit speaketh the truth and lieth not. Wherefore, it speaketh of things as they really are, and of things as they really will be; wherefore, these things are manifested unto us plainly, for the salvation of our souls. But behold, we are not witnesses alone in these things; for God also spake them unto prophets of old." (*See also* John 16:13; Romans 15:13; Moroni 18:26.)

Your Raise Came Through

Will a man rob God? Yet ye have robbed me. But ye say, Wherein have we robbed thee? In tithes and offerings.

Ye are cursed with a curse: for ye have robbed me, even this whole nation.

Bring ye all the tithes into the storehouse, that there may be meat in mine house, and prove me now herewith, saith the Lord of hosts, if I will not open you the windows of heaven, and pour you out a blessing, that there shall not be room enough to receive it.

Malachi 3:8–10

Mark had served a successful mission and was now back to the business of getting an education. He had no money saved to go to college, so he went to work part-time in a grocery store while he went to school. This provided the money he needed for his tuition and books.

Mark's testimony had been greatly strengthened while serving his mission. As he had shared his testimony with investigators about the truthfulness of certain gospel principles, his own testimony had grown. One principle that he firmly believed in was that of paying tithes and offerings to the Lord. But it wasn't until after his mission that this testimony was to be tried.

Fall quarter he was able to pay for his tuition and books and still had enough to pay his tithing. He even had some left over for spending money. But as winter quarter approached and tuition came due, Mark had just enough money to pay his tuition, and that was all. As the day he had to pay his tuition came closer, he started to debate the issue to himself. If he paid his tuition then he could not pay his tithing, but if he paid his tithing he would not be able to pay his tuition. Mark began to reason that the Lord wanted him to go to school and get an education. Since he was doing what the Lord wanted him to do, it would be all right not to pay his tithing right now. He could make it up later when he had a better paying job. This reasoning sounded logical, but it lacked one important thing. Mark could not get a spiritual confirmation that it was right. The Spirit kept whispering to his soul that he should pay his tithing even if it meant missing a quarter of school. So he went ahead and paid his tithing, which left him without enough money to pay his tuition —and just one week before the tuition was due.

The next week as Mark went to work, the assistant manager came to him and gave him a payroll check. He had already received his check and so he asked why he was receiving another one. The assistant manager replied that he didn't know why, but it had come and he was to give it to him. When Mark looked at the check, he saw it was for the amount he needed for his tuition. As he pressed the assistant manager to take back the check, he said, "No, it is yours. They sent it to you and you must take it."

Mark took the check and paid his tuition. The following week the manager came to him and told him that he had received the extra check because his raise had come through. When Mark asked, "What raise?" the manager said, "The one I put in for you." This was all news to Mark, but he was truly grateful, for he knew the true source of his help.

Teaching Ideas and Related Scriptures

Tithing: As we put the Lord first and pay our tithes and offerings, he will bless us both spiritually and temporally.

D&C 64:23. "Behold, now it is called today until the coming of the Son of Man, and verily it is a day of sacrifice, and a day for the tithing of my people; for he that is tithed shall not be burned at his coming." (*See also* Genesis 28:22; Malachi 3:8–10; 3 Nephi 24:8–10; D&C 119:4.)

The Car Was Going to Hit Him

And now, their preservation was astonishing to our whole army, yea, that they should be spared while there was a thousand of our brethren who were slain. And we do justly ascribe it to the miraculous power of God, because of their exceeding faith in that which they had been taught to believe—that there was a just God, and whosoever did not doubt, that they should be preserved by his marvelous power.

Alma 57:26

As a young boy, Tom grew up in Heber City, Utah. He enjoyed going to M.I.A., and was very involved in scouting. During the long cold winters in that mountain valley, the snow and ice would never melt off the roads from November through February.

One of the mischievous things the scouts did during the winter months was to "hook" cars. It was great fun to be pulled along the icy roads behind unsuspecting motorists.

Tom will never forget the night he hooked his first car. The roads seemed more icy and slick than usual. When he first hooked on, the driver knew it and tried to "shine him off" by swerving around on the ice. He finally threw him off and Tom went swirling down the road on his back, spinning like a top. When he came to a stop he was lying on his back very dizzy. As he looked back in the direction he had come, he saw another car speeding directly toward him. Tom felt helpless as he slipped and fell on the ice. Each time he struggled to get to his feet he fell again. The oncoming car got closer and closer until Tom knew that the car was unable to stop on the slick ice. He suddenly realized, with horror, that the car was going to hit him. Just as the car was about to strike him, Tom felt his body lifted up and thrown out of the path of the car. As he got up and dusted the snow off, he flexed his muscles and thought how great and strong he must be to throw himself from in front of the car. It wasn't until later, as he reflected over this terrifying experience, that he realized that his life had been spared that night by ministering angels.

Tom doesn't really know why the Lord intervened in his behalf. It could have been because of the faithful prayers of his family or because the Lord needed him to influence the lives of others. Tom does know, however, that the Lord did save his life that day and that he is here today because of divine intervention. Tom has since served as a mission president and a stake president and has influenced many lives for the better.

Teaching Ideas and Related Scriptures

Divine Protection: Tom learned firsthand that there are unseen forces working in our behalf. Although we cannot always see the results as easily as Tom did in this experience, most of us would be surprised to learn how often the Lord blesses and assists us in our lives.

Psalm 31:23. "O love the Lord, all ye his saints: for the Lord preserveth the faithful, and plentifully rewardeth the proud doer." (*See also* Alma 57; especially verse 26.)

Are Families Really Forever?

Behold, I stand at the door, and knock: if any man hear my voice, and open the door, I will come in to him, and will sup with him, and he with me.

Revelation 3:20

For as long as Elizabeth could remember she had been taught that "families are forever." She had always believed this without any doubt, that is until something happened that turned her life upside down.

It all started one day when her mother came to her and asked, "How would you feel if I told you I wanted to divorce your father." Elizabeth's first reaction was, "This isn't real. It has to be a bad dream. It can't be real!" Elizabeth looked at her mother and asked if she wanted an honest answer. Her mother said yes, so Elizabeth told her that she would be very hurt! The subject was dropped, but she could not get it off her mind. Her parents hadn't been happy together for years, but being a wishful teenager she had hoped it would all work out.

She went to her room crying and asked God, "Aren't families forever? If they are, show me a sign." No sign or immediate answer came. In fact, a few months later, her father told her that she had better start thinking of who she wanted to live with, because he and her mom were going to separate. All she could think about was, "How can I choose who to live with? I love both so much. I love my mother for her tenderness, and I love my father for his quiet support." She kept asking herself, "Aren't families forever? If so, why can't mine be?"

Often as Elizabeth went to bed, the main thought that kept going through her mind was, "What did I do wrong? If I was a better daughter this probably wouldn't be happening!"

One night as she fell asleep she had a dream. She found herself lost in a forest, holding on to a tree for comfort. She found
herself not wanting to let go because she was so scared. As she
was holding on to the tree, Christ came to her and asked, "Why
are you holding on to that tree? That tree cannot give you the
comfort that I can."

Elizabeth said, crying, "Lord, I cannot let go! I cannot! For I
am scared and lost. This tree will give me support!" The Lord
took her away from the tree and held her, which brought her
great joy and comfort. His love was sweeter than anything she
had ever experienced. His comfort was real! He walked her to a
small cottage and led her inside. She looked at him and asked,
"Lord, who do I belong to? I don't have a family." The Lord
looked at her lovingly and said, "My precious child, you belong
to me and the Father. This is our house and we want you to
know you belong here. We are your family."

As Elizabeth woke up her pillow was soaked with tears. She
felt that she understood the dream! The tree was the world,
which didn't bring real comfort. No matter how tight she held on
to it, it couldn't comfort her. She now understood that when
people turn to the Lord, they feel a comfort and a happiness that
the world doesn't know. Elizabeth had experienced a taste of
what pure joy is.

As time passed and Elizabeth tried to deal with the hurt and
confusion caused by her parent's separation, she started to
understand how the Lord offers his comfort to us. One evening
she went to the Lord in prayer, saying, "I need comfort, and
you have said that the scriptures have been written for us in
these latter-days. Please let me know where to read. I really
need comfort now." As she got up from her prayer, she threw
her scriptures onto her bed. They opened to Doctrine and Covenants 78:17–18, which reads: "Verily, verily, I say unto you, ye
are little children, and ye have not as yet understood how great
blessings the Father hath in his own hands and prepared for
you; and ye cannot bear all things now; nevertheless, be of good
cheer, for I will lead you along. The kingdom is yours and the
blessings thereof are yours, and the riches of eternity are
yours." It was then that she gained a testimony of the power
and comfort that the Lord offers us through the scriptures.

Elizabeth also learned that another source of comfort that Heavenly Father offers us is through friends. After sitting in church one day hurting inside over the problems with her family, she went out into the foyer. There she met a friend who asked how she was doing. As they talked the friend sensed that things were not well. They talked about the problem, and the friend explained to her how she could have an eternal family of her own and how right now through proper dating and right living she was setting the path to an eternal family. As they finished their conversation the friend hugged Elizabeth. At that moment she felt the same comfort and joy she had experienced in her dream.

Another source of comfort came to her as she attended her Church meetings. In her Laurel class they had a lesson on eternal marriage. Through that lesson she learned that if she desired an eternal family, she first would have to date wisely and be loving and Christlike. It also helped her to know what qualities to look for in choosing an eternal mate.

As Elizabeth worked through this troubled time in her life and discovered what great comfort Heavenly Father and Jesus Christ have to offer us, she came to understand better the scripture found in Revelation 3:20: "Behold, I stand at the door, and knock: if any man hear my voice, and open the door, I will come in to him, and will sup with him, and he with me."

Teaching Ideas and Related Scriptures

Comfort: Elizabeth received comfort as she turned to the Lord and let him help her.

John 14:18. "I will not leave you comfortless: I will come to you." (*See also* Isaiah 25:4; Romans 14:4; D&C 101:14.)

Dreams: One process by which we can receive help from the Lord is through dreams. The Lord used this method to instruct and comfort Elizabeth.

Joel 2:28. "And it shall come to pass afterward, that I will pour out my spirit upon all flesh; and your sons and your daughters shall prophesy, your old men shall dream dreams, your young men shall see visions."

Friends: Heavenly Father uses other people to comfort and help us in our times of need. Elizabeth was helped through a difficult time by a friend who was there when she needed her.

D&C 121:9. "Thy friends do stand by thee, and they shall hail thee again with warm hearts and friendly hands." (*See also* Proverbs 17:17.)

Prayer: Another source of comfort and guidance that helped Elizabeth with her problem was prayer.

Alma 37:37. "Counsel with the Lord in all thy doings, and he will direct thee for good; yea, when thou liest down at night lie down unto the Lord, that he may watch over you in your sleep; and when thou risest in the morning let they heart be full of thanks unto God; and if ye do these things, ye shall be lifted up at the last day." (*See also* Revelation 3:20.)

Patience: As we deal with problems as Elizabeth did, we must exercise patience as the Lord directs us.

D&C 78:17–18. "Verily, verily, I say unto you, ye are little children, and ye have not as yet understood how great blessings the Father hath in his own hands and prepared for you;

"And ye cannot bear all things now; nevertheless, be of good cheer, for I will lead you along. The kingdom is yours and the blessings thereof are yours, and the riches of eternity are yours." (*See also* Romans 15:4.)

Scriptures: Elizabeth turned to the scriptures and found instruction and comfort in dealing with her problem.

Romans 15:4. "For whatsoever things were written aforetime were written for our learning, that we through patience and comfort of the scriptures might have hope." (*See also* D&C 33:16.)

Why California?

And ye are called to bring to pass the gathering of mine elect; for mine elect hear my voice and harden not their hearts.

D&C 29:7

Sister Green received her mission call to the Los Angeles California mission. She had been taught that some missionaries are called to serve in certain areas because there are specific people in these areas that they can reach. Towards the end of her mission, she began to wonder if she had been called to serve in California for a specific reason. Many people she had taught had joined the Church, but she felt that they would have responded to any missionary that lived the mission rules and taught with the Spirit. She did not feel that any of them had joined specifically because of her.

She began to pray to her Father in Heaven to find out if there was a special reason why she had been called to the Los Angeles area. She wondered if there were specific people whom she had been sent to find and whether she had found these people.

A few weeks later, a heavy rain storm moved into the area. After phone tracting for three days without much success, Sister Green and her companion decided to do some door-to-door tracting in spite of the weather. They prayerfully selected an area in which to tract and set out to find someone to teach. They tracted for several hours with no success. Either the people weren't home or they were not enthused about letting two wet missionaries come into their homes and drip all over their furniture and carpet.

Even though they were soaked and it was getting late, they decided they should finish the street they were on before return-

107

ing to their apartment to get ready for their evening appointments. When they knocked at the last house on the street, a woman in her midthirties named Pam answered the door. When they introduced themselves the lady did not say a word but just stood there and stared intently at Sister Green. When they asked her if they could come in, she did not answer but continued to stare. Finally she invited them to come in out of the rain.

As they talked with Pam, they found out that she had an eleven-year-old daughter and a three-month-old baby boy. The missionaries asked if they could return and have a family home evening with them.

When Sister Green and her companion returned a few nights later, they had a very good experience. Pam liked the family home evening so well that they challenged her to take the missionary discussions. She readily accepted.

During the second discussion Sister Green found out why she had been sent to California. Sister Green was not with her companion but was teaching with a Relief Society sister from the local ward. They were teaching about the plan of salvation, and Pam was really interested in the premortal existence. When Pam learned that all of us lived with Heavenly Father before we were born, she became very excited and said that this doctrine explained so much to her. She told them that she had had a dream before her son was born. In her dream, she was in the hospital and saw someone holding out a little baby to her. The baby was very small and pretty and had dark hair. She could see the baby's face very clearly and the arms of the person holding the baby. She then saw the baby as a grown man and heard a voice, which she felt was the voice of the Lord, telling her that someday her baby would be a man of God. This is how her dream had ended.

Pam then explained that after her baby had been born, as she was lying on her hospital bed, the doctor held her baby out to her in exactly the same way that it had happened in her dream. It was the same baby and the same arms holding him in exactly the same way. Pam said that she now understood how she could see her baby even before he was born.

The Relief Society sister with Sister Green told Pam how special this experience was and indicated that some people even see their missionaries before they knock on their door. Pam, with tears in her eyes, looked at Sister Green and said that she knew that this was true because she had seen Sister Green several years ago in a dream.

In her dream, Sister Green knocked at her door and, when she opened it, she heard a voice say, "I knocked at your door as a beggar and you turned me away." Pam had always felt that this was the voice of the Savior.

When Sister Green really did knock on her door, because of this dream, Pam could not turn her away. The Spirit then indicated to Sister Green that teaching Pam was one of the reasons she had been called to California to serve her mission.

Many times since that day, Sister Green has wondered what would have happened if she had decided not to serve a mission. Pam may not have responded to anyone else. She has always felt grateful for the confidence that the Lord demonstrated in her by placing her in Pam's dream years before she went on her mission. This experience strengthened her testimony that mission calls really are made under inspiration.

Teaching Ideas and Related Scriptures

Missionary Work; Mission Calls Are Inspired: This is one of numerous stories that indicate that the Lord directs the missionary program and sends missionaries where they can do the most good or where they need to serve most in order to be prepared for future calls in the Church. It would also be good to use this story to emphasize how important it is to serve a mission, because there may be someone who will only respond to a particular person, approach, or personality.

D&C 123:12. "For there are many yet on the earth among all sects, parties, and denominations, who are blinded by the subtle craftiness of men, whereby they lie in wait to deceive, and who are only kept from the truth because they know not where to find it." (*See also* D&C 18:15–16; D&C 29:7.)

Revelation and Dreams: This story can be used to illustrate that dreams are one way revelation from God can be received. When teaching stories from scriptures in which the Lord spoke in dreams, you can use this story as a modern-day example of that process.

1 Nephi 2:2. "And it came to pass that the Lord commanded my father, even in a dream, that he should take his family and depart into the wilderness." (*See also* Genesis 37 [Joseph as a boy]; Genesis 40 [Joseph in prison]; Genesis 41 [Joseph and Pharaoh]; 1 Kings 3:5–14 [Solomon]; Matthew 1:20–24 [Joseph]; Matthew 2 [wise men and Joseph].)

Subject Index

Subject Index

Scripture Index

OLD TESTAMENT

NEW TESTAMENT

Scripture Index

DOCTRINE AND COVENANTS